The Republic of Venice and Republic of Genoa: Rivals and their Mediterranean

By Charles River Editors

Didier Descouens' picture of the *Porta Magna* at the Venetian Arsenal

About Charles River Editors

Charles River Editors provides superior editing and original writing services across the digital publishing industry, with the expertise to create digital content for publishers across a vast range of subject matter. In addition to providing original digital content for third party publishers, we also republish civilization's greatest literary works, bringing them to new generations of readers via ebooks.

Sign up here to receive updates about free books as we publish them, and visit Our Kindle Author Page to browse today's free promotions and our most recently published Kindle titles.

Introduction

View of the Entrance to the Arsenal by Canaletto, 1732

Venice and Genoa

"As in the Arsenal of the Venetians

Boils in winter the tenacious pitch

To smear their unsound vessels over again

For sail they cannot; and instead thereof

One makes his vessel new, and one recaulks

The ribs of that which many a voyage has made

One hammers at the prow, one at the stern

This one makes oars and that one cordage twists

Another mends the mainsail and the mizzen…" – Dante's *Inferno*

The mystical floating city of Venice has inspired awe for generations, and it continues to be one of the most visited European cities for good reason. Tourists are drawn to the stunning blend of classical, Gothic, and Renaissance-inspired architecture across the picturesque towns and villages, the charming open-air markets, the mouthwatering traditional cuisine, and of course, the famous gondolas drifting down the twinkling blue waters. While these gondolas, along with the time-honored models of the Venetian vessels docked in the harbors, are one of the city's most defining landmarks, their beginnings are shrouded in a more obscure part of Venetian history.

To the first settlers of the unpromising, marshy islands of Venice in the 5th century BCE, it appeared as if any attempt at civilization was doomed to fail. Yet, even with the cards stacked against them, the artful inhabitants mastered the unlivable terrain and slowly pieced together a society that would put the small, unassuming city right on the map. In time, the city evolved into the most powerful maritime empire in all of Europe.

Founded in the wake of the decline of the Roman Empire, the Republic of Venice lasted for more than a thousand years, from 697-1797, and in order to understand its singular position in world history, it is necessary to first note its geographical positioning and its topographical make-up: Located in northeastern Italy at the head of the Adriatic, the city is made up of 120 islands that are connected by 430 bridges that cross over 170 canals, referred to as a "rio" or plural "rii" (Italian for river). As a maritime power, the interests of Venice once reached all the way to Asia, which allowed it to form an important crossroads within the Eastern Mediterranean, in terms of trade. In Venice, a vast array of products (raw materials, spices, cloth) came all the way from North Africa, Russia, and India and were exchanged for the goods and wealth of Europe."[1]

Aside from the sheer size of the Venetian Empire and its long duration, it is no exaggeration to say that Venice was a city-state like no other in the world. Since it was not surrounded by an extensive rural area, it could not simply live off the bounty of the land, as others commonly did. Instead, the Venetians were forced to rely solely upon their entrepreneurial trade and their ingenuity; these essential collective characteristics contributed in no small way to the success of the city. In fact, this lack of dependence on a rural area ended up being a significant advantage because it ensured the city needed to develop many of the characteristics of an industrial revolution several centuries before the actual Industrial Revolution began in Britain. Moreover, in order to handle (and multiply) its bountiful financial prosperity, the Venetian Republic also invented one of the earliest banking systems in the world, and while the Tuscan city of Florence is usually referred to as the Athens of Renaissance Italy thanks to its position at the center of learning, art, and culture, some scholars would argue that Venice has a far better claim to that prestigious mantle.[2]

---

[1] James H.S. McGregor, *Venice from the Ground Up.* (Cambridge, MA: The Belknap Press of Harvard University Press, 2006), 2.
[2] Wills, 13.

Venice, of course, earned its remarkable reputation on its own merit, but the reason for its current fame should be credited at least in part to its status as one of the most important tourist destinations of all time, attracting travelers interested in religion, art, culture, architecture, the seashore as well as shopping. As far back as the 16th century, pilgrims flocked there to take in its numerous holy sites, the remnants of the city's medieval heritage, and in the 17th century, rich northern Europeans flocked to the city as part of their lengthy Grand Tour, hoping to feast their eyes on the unusual cityscape and its unique cultural heritage. Many of those famous writers penned unforgettable accounts of the city in English and in German, stories that only served to increase its fortunes over time.[3]

As one of the most famous cities of all ages, it is not hard to agree upon Venice's prominence in world history. However, in making this natural acceptance, it is easy to overlook the sheer improbability of its existence. Somehow, a marshy, deserted archipelago became the second largest city in all of Europe, with territorial holdings spanning all across the Mediterranean Sea, by the 13th century.

Such is the awesome power of the city that a "Myth of Venice" has dominated scholarly circles, a romanticizing that the city actively cultivated in order to construct its own identity.[4] The Venetians obviously embraced the myth to show the city in its best light, but there was also a negative side to it - in juxtaposition with the tolerant, open, benevolent city, there was a representation of Venice as repressive, governed by a decadent and secretive ruling class of elites.[5]

As positive and negative threads intertwine, unraveling the myth is proving to be a challenge. Today, as historians work to understand the extent of the gap between the myth and the reality of Venice, they reveal numerous contradictions, as well as subtle revisions and outright manipulations in the historical record. Of course, as they do so, they often unconsciously reproduce either the same myth or antimyth that was propagated for centuries.[6] At the same time, they cannot help but try to explain the Republic's apparently unique, thousand-year success.[7]

In a country that is as crowded with famous cities as Italy, Genoa is usually not one that first leaps to mind, at least for an English-speaking audience. If Venice, Florence, and Rome are the

---

[3] On the Grand Tour, see Bruce Redford, *Venice and the Grand Tour* (New Haven, CT: Yale University Press, 1996), as well as Manfred Pfister and Barbara Schaff, eds, *Venetian Views, Venetian Blinds: English Fantasies of Venice* (Amsterdam, Netherlands: Rodopi, 1999).
[4] Wills defines the myth of Venice as "that historical romance the city told about itself to prove that it was set apart from ordinary states," Wills, 20. Rosand explains the "myth of Venice" in a less benevolent way, writing, "That collective image—of the self-proclaimed Most Serene Republic as an ideal political entity whose ruling patriciate were selflessly devoted to the commonwealth—has come to be known as the 'myth of Venice,'" David Rosand, *Venice. The Figuration of a State* (Chapel Hill, NC: University of North Carolina Press, 2005), 1.
[5] Martin and Romano, "Reconsidering Venice," 2-3. According to Martin and Romano, this antimyth was produced as a result of Venice's incursions on the Italian mainland, 3.
[6] Martin and Romano, "Reconsidering Venice," 4-6.
[7] Rosand, 4.

top three, they are often followed by Pisa, Sienna, and Naples, not to mention the islands of Sardinia and Sicily. Indeed, Genoa would come towards the end of a much longer list, and it might be most closely associated with its famous native son, Christopher Columbus, who ultimately sailed for Spain. For avid tourists, Genoa might be the port of call for those wishing to visit the stunning Cinque Terre on the Ligurian coast nearby, and for an expert in world politics, the city of Genoa might recall the memories of the tragic events of the 27th G8 summit in July 2001, when, at the height of the anti-globalization movement, protests turned violent and resulted in the death of a 23-year-old Carlo Giuliani. In today's news, Genoa might represent Italy's crumbling infrastructure and the apparent powerlessness of its government to repair it - on Tuesday, August 14, 2018, one of the main bridges of the city, the Morandi Bridge, collapsed, killing 43 people and leaving 600 homeless. The bridge's demise also destroyed Italy's reputation as an expert in mechanical engineering.

Although Genoa cannot compete in the popular imagination with some of Italy's more famous cities, this busy port town perched above the sea once boasted a powerful empire that rivaled that of Venice. It also lasted for roughly the same time period, rising in the early Middle Ages and coming to an end at the hands of Napoleon Bonaparte near the end of the 18th century. Beyond its own success, the city's position at the head of the Mediterranean gave it an important strategic location from which to observe Italian and European history, as well as the world beyond. Today, historians are starting to correct the imbalance that has focused on Venice, Florence and Rome, and new histories are gradually introducing Genoa to the world, even as much remains to be uncovered.

The Republic of Venice and Republic of Genoa: The History of the Italian Rivals and their Mediterranean Empires looks at the origins of the cities, their rise to power across the Mediterranean, and their inevitable demises. Along with pictures of important people, places, and events, you will learn about Venice and Genoa like never before.

The Republic of Venice and Republic of Genoa: The History of the Italian Rivals and their Mediterranean Empires

About Charles River Editors

Introduction

- Venice's Origins
- Genoa's Origins
- Genoa and the First Crusade
- The Start of an Empire
- Genoa and the Late Middle Ages
- The End of the Middle Ages
- Genoa's Golden Age
- The Decline of Venice
- The Decline of Genoa's Republic
- Online Resources
- Bibliography

Free Books by Charles River Editors

Discounted Books by Charles River Editors

Venice's Origins

Italy is one of the most recognizable countries in the world. Shaped like a boot that kicks the triangular ball of Sicily across the Mediterranean, Italy is home to some of the most distinctive cities, not just in Europe, but in the entire world: Naples, Florence and Rome, just to name three. However, of all these singular places, Venice is often considered the most remarkable of all, thanks in large part to the Republic of Venice bringing the region to life halfway through the 1st millennium CE.[8] The English writer Evelyn Waugh put this sentiment of Venice's exceptionality rather eloquently, noting, "If every museum in the New World were emptied, if every famous building in the Old World were destroyed and only Venice saved, there would be enough there to fill a full lifetime with delight. Venice, with all its complexity and variety, is in itself the greatest surviving work of art in the world."[9]

Indeed, a full historical account of Venice's sophisticated, lucrative trade empire paints one impressive picture of the city. Its intense naval battles (which fortunately tended to take place *abroad* and not on their home soil) also provides an impressive version of Venice, as did its internal affairs. Indeed, a relative lack of rebellion within city politics allowed Venice to earn its boastful nickname *Serenissima*, and by keeping to itself, it was truly "Most undisturbed."[10]

Added to these different elements, there is also Venice's cultural production to take into consideration, including artists, musicians and writers from Giovanni Bellini, Andrea Palladio and Veronica Franco to Carlo Goldoni, Veronica Franco and Antonio Vivaldi. It's also important to note the prominence of Padua, a town under Venetian control since the early 1400s and home to one of the world's most prominent universities.

Venice is rightly also associated with a feeling of bewilderment due to the fact it's a floating city with canals in place of roads. A place that seems to defy descriptions, even scholars who embark on histories of Venice remark that it simultaneously inspires an endless amount of words about its waters, its stones, its colors, and smells, while at the same time acknowledging that the place invites silence. After all, what else could there be to say about one of the most frequently discussed cities in the world?[11] Among the most evocative definitions of the floating city, the famous Venetian writer Tiziano Scarpa described Venice as a "fish," with its watery backbone being the Grand Canal - crossed by four different bridges - and the smaller canals being its skeleton.[12] The crime novelist Reginald Hill called the famous Piazza San Marco a "giraffe - absurd, impossible, and beautiful beyond computation, as if Michelangelo, Christopher Wren, Walt Disney and God had sat on a committee to build it."[13] William Shakespeare was also

---

[8] Crouzet-Pavan, "Il Rinascimento."
[9] Gary Wills *Venice: Lion City: The Religion of Empire.* (New York: Simon and Schuster, 2013), 11.
[10] Wills, 12.
[11] Crouzet-Pavan, *Venice Triumphant,* ix.
[12] Elizabeth Horodowich. *A Brief History of Venice: A New History of the City and Its People.* (New York: Little Brown Book Group, 2013), 6.
[13] Richard J.B., Bosworth *Italian Venice: A History.* (New Haven, CT: Yale University Press, 2014), xi.

enamored with Venice, and he set a few of his most famous plays in the Republican city, including the tragedy *The Merchant of Venice*.[14] In many ways, to understand Venice it might be most efficient to simply pick a favorite version of the city and embrace it.

The Venetian Empire is bookended by the fortunes of other empires, starting with the fall of the Roman Empire and ending with the rise of Napoleon Bonaparte and the Austrian Empire of the Hapsburgs.

When Attila the Hun and his men terrorized the vibrant Italian town of Altinum in 452 CE, those who managed to dodge the Huns' maces, swords, and lances hastily bagged up their essentials and hauled their behinds to the unoccupied outskirts of the lagoon. The scattering Celtic inhabitants, otherwise known as the "Veneti," sought refuge in the marshy islands of Iesolo, Torcello, and Malamoco. Initially, the escapees hoped that the relocation would be temporary, but the door of this likelihood swung to a close.

The Veneti had seen the extent of the destruction inflicted upon the Italian mainland by the recent wave of Hun and Germanic raids, and they knew they could no longer return to their beloved homeland. And thus, the fledgling city of Venice, or in Italian, the "Civitas Rivoalti," was born.

Not much is known about the origins of these native peoples. In a famous letter written by the Roman statesman Cassiodorus from 537-538 in which he describes the maritime population, he emphasized the instability of the landscape, which he describes as "liquid plains" with its brackish waters, silk and reeds. The letter notes that these peoples were fishermen, salt miners and transporters, who had already formed a small but nonetheless functional economy. Although quite poor, they were a self-sufficient and peaceful people.[15] Some argue that these natives represented an independent culture, while others claim they had been influenced by the cultural traditions of the ancient Roman Empire.[16] What is known for certain is that the arrival of so many fleeing newcomers served as a transformative catalyst for change. In addition to irrevocably altering the social structure of the original Venetians, they set into motion the inexorable process that would lead to the founding of the Republic of Venice.[17]

According to one famous myth, Venice sprang to life at the stroke of noon on Friday March 25, 421, with the creation of the San Giacomo church, a myth that actually anticipated the truth by around 400 years.[18] Another myth suggests that Venice was founded long before that by the defeated Trojans who were fleeing the destruction of their city. However, today the generally

---

[14] See Graham Holderness, *Shakespeare and Venice* (Burlington, VT: Ashgate Publishing Ltd., 2010).
[15] Crouzet-Pavan, *Venice Triumphant*, 5.
[16] Longworth, 72
[17] Longworth, 76; see also Lane 4.
[18] John Julius Norwich. *Venice: The Rise to Empire.* (London: Allen Lane, 1977), 28-29. See also Nicol, Donald M. Nicol Byzantium and Venice: A Study in Diplomatic and Cultural Relations. (Cambridge, MA: Cambridge University Press, 1992), 2.

accepted hypothesis is that in 568, the Lombard (Germanic) invasion of northern Italy inspired a migration of refugees from the mainland cities, provoking the occupants of the coastal plain to find a new place to settle.[19] The 3 miles of water surrounding Venice was akin to the world's largest moat, for the invaders were said to have had no ships, and knew little to nothing about navigating the unpredictable waters. The Venetians were safe – at least, for then. Altinum has since sunk to the ground and is now classified as a lost city – today, it is nothing more than a 100-hectare patch populated by stalks of corn and soybean plants just north of the Venetian airport.

A 17th century depiction of the San Marco basin in Venice

As that suggests, when Venice's first new settlers began to build their new city, they were choosing this unusual spot not because they relished the idea of living on an unstable marsh, but because they needed a place where they could be free.[20] What's more, historians agree that most likely they only intended to be there in the short-term, but regardless of their original intentions, the lagoon's inhospitality proved quite useful to the asylum seekers, who found a space for themselves without fearing excessive competition.[21] The only requirement was that they familiarize themselves with their unusual new environment in order to survive and eventually thrive.[22]

---

[19] Lane 4; see also Longworth, 2.
[20] Madden, *Venice: A New History*, 1.
[21] Longworth, 2.
[22] Longworth, 2.

One of the first issues the new settlers had to deal with was the problem of fresh water. On the one hand, the brininess of the lagoon was of great value to Venice, as it had offered the people one of their first major industrial operations: salt mining. On the other hand, they were desperately in need of freshwater for drinking, an ironic situation for a people who were quite literally up to their necks in water. At the time, the only actual source of fresh water was rainfall from the sky, and in order to be able to depend on it, the Venetians had to systematize its collection in a formal manner.[23] Thus, it is important to remember that Venice, despite hosting a culture that relied on boats for daily activities, also needed to create a hydraulic system and a rigorous social discipline in order to overcome its unnatural physical environment and harness it for everyone's ultimate benefit.[24]

Though they constantly struggled with the shifting landscape, the Venetians proved to be up to the challenge.[25] They managed to make the most of their unusual environment by creating a symbiotic way of life once they were safely out of reach of potential Lombard overlords.[26] They had to perform back-breaking labor in order to consolidate the shorelines, and they had dredge the swamps in order to erect structures atop it. In order to build these ingenious buildings, they had to gather whatever precarious materials they could scavenge, until they were able to transport bricks and stones from the mainland.[27]

Moreover, as they modified the lagoon, the lagoon in turn worked to shape their character and their collective identity. The Venetian people were an ethnically diverse group thanks to the constant influx of traders and invaders, but, because of their harsh circumstances, they ended up forging a common identity. To this day, Venetians are known as a determined people who bonded together in the face of their shared adversity.[28]

One of their other defining characteristics was their religiosity. Venice's earliest churches, inspired by the Byzantine's Eastern Orthodox religion, show signs of being enlarged multiple times, suggesting that the churchgoing community was developing at a rapid speed.[29] Beyond the practical shaping of their collective character, the act of building a city out of a lagoon became an important part of the "myth of Venice" that was already being formed in its earliest days.[30]

In the first century of the history of Venice, the "city" could not be properly defined as such; at this point, it was essentially a group of communities with loose political ties. Each of these communities belonged in the powerful orbit of the Byzantines, and starting in 584, the Byzantines formed these communities into a *ducato* (a duchy). They were affiliated with

---

[23] Wills, 18.
[24] Wills, 19.
[25] Crouzet-Pavan, *Venice Triumphant,* 8-9.
[26] McGregor, 1.
[27] Crouzet-Pavan, *Venice Triumphant,* 9.
[28] Ferraro, 2-3.
[29] Crouzet-Pavan, *Venice Triumphant,* 9.
[30] Rosand, 2.

Ravenna, a prosperous coastal city to the south of Venice in today's region of Emilia Romagna. It was not for another 100 years that Venice "proper" came to be, so the earliest date that scholars recognize as its start is 697.

At this time, the Byzantines made the many individual lagoons into a separate military command, ruled under an elected "dux" (in Italian *doge*). The first doge was named Paoluccio Anafesto.[31] Around that time, the lagoon area began its slow process of unification, as the Byzantine authorities started to establish a new administrative district for the area.[32] Then, over the course of the 7th century, the communities of refugees on the individual Venetian islands began to develop into permanent settlements. Amongst them, their leading families began to evolve their own political and administrative institutions.[33] However, it was not until 751 that Ravenna finally fell and relinquished its power over Venice definitively, marking the start of the city's own autonomy.

Two further events proved important for the consolidation of the Venetian territory and forging the identity of its people. First, in 810, the regional governor appointed by the Byzantine emperor relocated to the site of the city, which served as a clear signal of its burgeoning political importance. Now this confederation of islands had a new capital, which sent a flood of laborers and soldiers in order to build up and fortify the city. The influx of population into the urban center had the effect of emptying out the surrounding areas, further shifting the demographic balance of power in favor of Venice.[34]

This crucial bureaucratic move was soon compounded by an event of tantamount symbolic significance that helped form the city's identity and influenced its iconography: the arrival of Saint Mark's body. Today, when people visit Venice, everywhere they turn they encounter images of lions, strutting or skulking, enormous or tiny, calm or threatening. The reason lions are in Venice is because of their association with Saint Mark, the patron saint of Venice, but the reason why Saint Mark reached Venice is profoundly connected to the formation of the Republic.[35] In life, Mark had no actual geographical connection to Venice, and he had actually been buried in Alexandria, Egypt, but in 829 Venetian merchants stole the body of Mark from its sepulcher under the pretext that Muslims were about to desecrate the relic.[36] The merchants brought his body to the city, where he was joyously celebrated by the proud, religious people.[37] This act of thievery caused Saint Theodore to be displaced as its patron saint.[38]

---

[31] Lane, 4-5.
[32] Longworth, 7.
[33] Nicol, 9.
[34] Crouzet-Pavan, *Venice Triumphant*, 10.
[35] Wills, 27.
[36] Wills, 29. See also, Lane, 88.
[37] Lane, 88. Like most Italians, the Venetians were of the Catholic faith, but their religious beliefs and practices were specifically linked to their politics. Much like they did with everything, they kept their religion at a firm distance from the papal and Byzantine forms of faith. Wills, 14.
[38] This date marks the founding of the Basilica of San Marco, which was consecrated in 832, in order to house the

As they did with everything of importance to them, the Venetian people capitalized on their possession of Saint Mark's body, which served as a divine indication of their independence from other peoples and other cities. Thanks to the arrival of Saint Mark, the political power that Venice acquired in 810 was bolstered by its newfound theological power, and the strong ties of faith and patriotism helped hold together the entire precarious concept of the lagoon city.[39] These twin forces helped to focus and to drive the development of the quickly growing Republic.[40]

The Venetians were not deterred by the uneven and often waterlogged terrains of the unfamiliar territory. On the contrary, they not only adjusted to, but mastered the nautical lifestyle and the aquaculture that came with it, slowly but surely evolving into the prestigious naval powerhouse it would one day become. Despite its size, the republic would become the envy of all the shipping and armory industries worldwide, dominating these fields against all odds.

For a time, Venice was known as the "Serenissima Repubblica di Venezia," or in English, the "Very Serene One." To those outside, at its height, Venice was the picture of peace. Absent were the political turmoil and economic instability affecting those in European cities, both neighboring and distant. Its proficiency in maritime trade brought prosperity and lifted the republic from obscurity, but more importantly, created a community where members of all classes seemed to coexist in harmony. At the same time, while the Venetians were far from aggressive, they were anything but pushovers. It became common knowledge that the Venetians were not to be trifled with, for they could easily resort to violence – and beyond – when the situation called for it. The Venetians were always capable of looking after themselves, as evidenced by the first inhabitants. The enterprising folks found a creative solution to outsmart what was once seen as unlivable terrain. As Leonardo da Vinci would later say, "Simplicity is the ultimate sophistication."

First, an impenetrable barrier constructed out of wooden planks and pilings were built along the canal to keep the water out. To build a solid foundation on the space between the small and marshy islands, millions of thick wooden stakes about 4 meters long apiece were submerged underwater and firmly hammered into the sea bed. The closely-packed stakes shored up a man-made bed of either hardened clay or another wooden platform that could support the weight of each structure.

The Santa Maria Della Salute Church in the Dorsoduro region of Venice was said to have required a total of 1,106,657 stakes alone. This unconventional construction method was a

---

Saint's remains. See Henry Maguire and Robert S. Nelson, Eds, *San Marco, Byzantium, and The Myths of Venice* (Washington, DC: Dumbarton Oaks Research Library and Collection, 2010). Chambers notes that although San Marco was the spiritual patron of the empuire, by the 16th century there were also ancient gods involved in its iconography. Perhaps not surprisingly, Mercury and Neptune, the gods of commerce and the sea, appear as the patrons of Venice in art. D.S. Chambers, *The Imperial Age of Venice* (1380-1580). (London: Harcourt Brace Jovanovich, inc., 1970), 33.

[39] Wills, 15.
[40] McGregor, 1.

painstaking process, as the wood had to be obtained and delivered from the forests of Montenegro, Croatia, and Slovenia. As for the buildings, brick was mostly used, for they were cheap, easily made, and one of the lightest, but most resilient materials available.

The Santa Maria Della Salute Church

Why use wood, when steel or metal rods were far more superior in durability? For starters, ancient Venetians used oak or larch, which were believed to be the most water-resistant of their kind. While wood is usually not immune to rot caused by water and oxygen contact, the absence of the latter underwater prevented the growth of harmful fungi or bacteria, keeping the wood in nearly pristine condition. Moreover, the nonstop flow of the salty water of the Venetian lagoons, coupled with the silt and soil it brought with it, petrified the wood, creating a stone-like and virtually immovable base that lasted for over 5 centuries.

Early Venetians would also use the dubious terrain they were given to their advantage. As the marshlands were clearly unsuitable for farming, the Venetians trained themselves to become fishermen. Sea creatures, mostly fish, were their only source of nourishment for a time. For fresh water, Venetians found a solution in implanting wells and small drains into the center of each community square. The rainwater collected in the wells was stowed away in underground tanks that filtered the water with sand.

As a result, fish became so valuable that it became a type of early Venetian currency. Bundles of fish in varying amounts were swapped in exchange for wheat, wood, and wine. To this day, the multifaceted art of and inherent appreciation of fishery runs deep in the locals' veins.

While fish was used as a type of local currency, salt was commonly used when trading with the mainland or with those overseas. Salt rations were also a mode of payment preferred by ancient Roman soldiers, which was known as "salarium argentum," later inspiring the English word, "salary."

Though there was no shortage of salt on the island, actually procuring the product was a challenge. Back then, this was a task entrusted to the handful of Benedictine monasteries around the lagoon. Italians learned from the ways of Ancus Martin, one of the Roman kings, who introduced a salt-making technique that involved allowing sea water into an enclosed reservoir. The sea water baked under the sun, which then evaporated to form a treasury of brine. The raw brine was later poured into shallow, iron pans and the water boiled off. The glittering salt crystals were then scraped out, and the process repeated. Nonetheless, the Venetians would not only improve their ways, they soon excelled in the practice. At the height of local salt production in the 1200s, there were at least 119 saltworks in Venice.

Genoa's Origins

Liguria, the northwest region of Italy of which Genoa is capital, is one of the smallest regions of Italy, at 5,405 square kilometers or about 2,087 square miles, which makes it just a little bit bigger than Delaware.[41] In painting a rather vivid picture of Liguria, the journalist Nicholas Walton described its shape a "mountainous slug that sits over the lid of the Mediterranean like the moustache on the cruel top lip of a South American dictator."[42] Nestled on the belly of that mountainous slug, Genoa is positioned towards the sea and is surrounded on all sides by steep hills and mountains. Perhaps some of the drama of the city was born out of the fact that it feels like an amphitheater centered around the port, which serves as its watery stage.[43]

The origins of the Republic of Genoa begin with that sea and the mountains that hem it in.[44] The words that writers most often evoke when describing the unique topography of Genoa are dramatic, stunning, rugged, hostile, and unforgiving.[45] If it is precisely these rugged cliffs and rocky beaches that have held the power to entrance travelers for generations, the downside of such dramatic terrain is that life was not particularly easy for the Genoese, who had to make do

---

[41] Epstein, 10.
[42] Walton, *Genoa, "La Superba,"* 5.
[43] Thomas Allison Kirk, *Genoa and the Sea: Policy and Power in an Early Modern Maritime Republic, 1559–1684* (Baltimore, MD: The Johns Hopkins University Press, 2013), 3.
[44] Benes, "Introduction," 1.
[45] Kirk, 3.

with poor mountain soils and deal with unpredictable, unnavigable rivers.[46] In fact, aside from the Mediterranean Sea, the city's topography is also determined by its relationship with the two rivers that mark its natural boundaries on either side. The Bisagno and the Polcevera reach the sea on the east and the west sides of the city, serving to limit the territorial expansion of the city itself. These two rivers cut Genoa off from all of its surrounding territory, but they did have the useful function of carving out mountain passes leading to Piedmont, Lombardy, the Po Valley, and the major Alpine passes. Another strategic element of Genoa's location is that its position at the northern most point of the Tyrrhenian Sea provides the city with the shortest land route from the western Mediterranean to northern Italy, as well as the closest Tyrrhenian port for those coming from the north. This meant it was favored by those interested in commerce or in travel.[47]

Due to these geographical constraints, the city of Genoa itself was destined to remain a thin strip of territory, so while the Genoese were able to make inroads all over the known world, they only conquered a bit of land immediately to the north.[48] One of the many miracles of Genoa - and a true testament to its people - is that it was able to become such a dominant power with precious little flat land to its name.[49]

Although Genoa marks the shortest overland route between the western Mediterranean and northern Italy, it was not the easiest means of travel by any stretch. The mountains of the Riviera of Liguria are rather steep and totally barren. Their watershed is quite close to the coast, which means that rivers are able to change size completely depending on the season. In the spring and autumn, there might be a raging torrent, while in the summer, there might be a totally dry creek bed in its place.[50] This unpredictability means that no permanent structures could be built in and around the rivers, and moreover, it meant that all travel routes had to be governed by the season and thus could not be relied upon year-round. Unlike the rivers of northeastern Italy that Venetians were able to navigate with ease, the rivers around Genoa refused to offer the Genoese the same advantage. Thus, during the times when weather conditions made it possible to travel and transport goods to Genoa, it was necessary to use a train of mules. Compounding all these difficulties, Genoa also lacked a fertile climate, the very type of environment in which large cities usually spring up.[51]

Nonetheless, Genoa did enjoy several advantages compared to other cities that were developing at the same time. The first had to do with its water supplies - unlike the Republic of Venice, which had to invent hydraulics to make its brackish water drinkable, Genoa did have natural supplies of drinkable water.[52] The area also had weak coastal currents and compatible

---

[46] Epstein, 9-10.
[47] Kirk, 3.
[48] Kirk, 5.
[49] Epstein, 9.
[50] Kirk, 4.
[51] Kirk, 5.
[52] Epstein, 10.

prevailing winds that made for clear sailing both south and east, the key directions for the Genoese as they set about building their empire.[53]

In order to understand how an exceptional Republic could have been founded on a tiny, hostile strip of land, it is necessary to know a little bit about the people responsible for these remarkable, resourceful feats of engineering. When Italian cities get paired up with the seven deadly sins, as is wont to happen in a Catholic country with highly individualistic cities, Genoa is associated with pride or vainglory.[54] Venice was referred to as *La Serenissima* ("Most Undisturbed"), and Genoa was known as *La Superba* ("The Proud"). Pride is the most common of all recurring themes of scholarship on the Republic of Genoa, forming a thread that weaves throughout the historiography. The physical city itself is often described as proud, and so too is it depicted as regal and as confident.[55]

This legendary Genoese pride come to explain the remarkable patriotism of the people and their commitment to liberty, which might appear somewhat ironic considering the city's long dependence on slave labor.[56] However, if one takes into consideration that liberty, in Genoa, meant liberty to conduct business,[57] the dependence on slavery within the Republic and the people's acceptance of that seeming paradox becomes easier to interpret.

When viewed from the perspective of today, it also might seem to be in open contradiction with another well-known trait of the Genoese people: their piety. However, colonial attitudes at the time used religion and the promise of redemption as a justification for slavery, making the two not just compatible but actually symbiotic.

At the time of the founding of the city, the pride of the inhabitants was, no doubt, essential for them to perform the impossible task of creating a viable society on an unapologetically inhospitable tract of land. Nonetheless, the reputation came with a significant downside still visible in their legacy today, because the proud Genoese are also associated with negative qualities of individualism and clannishness. This meant that the city was plagued by internal conflicts that often weakened them vis-à-vis the outsiders who wanted to take over. It also meant that in the context of a port city which had a huge amount of diverse peoples coming and going, this clannishness only subsided insofar as the Genoese people were open to outsiders when they felt they could coopt their talent for their benefit.[58]

---

[53] Epstein, 10.
[54] Epstein, xv.
[55] Antonio Musarra, *Genova e il mare nel Medioevo* (Bologna: Il mulino, 2015), 9.
[56] See Giustina Olgiati and Andrea Zappia, *Schiavi. A Genova e in Liguria* (Genoa: SAGEP, 2018).
[57] On the importance of liberty in Genoese culture, see Matteo Salonia, *Genoa's Freedom: Entrepreneurship, Republicanism, and the Spanish Atlantic* (Lanham, MD: Lexington Books, 2017), xvi and
and Christine Shaw, "Concepts of *Libertà* in Renaissance Genoa," in Communes and Despots in Medieval and Renaissance Italy, ed. John E. Law and Bernadette Paton (Farnham: Ashgate, 2010), 177-190.
[58] Epstein, xiv–xv. See also, Robert S. Lopez, "Genoa," in *Dictionary of the Middle Ages*, n.d. Epstein clarifies: The
    people of Genoa were happy to welcome with open arms the people that they saw as beneficial and pushed out or
    mistreated those who were not—a rather standard practice, in those days as in today's. Epstein, *Genoa and the*

As they made the land of Genoa viable and simultaneously managed to expand their empire across the Ligurian and Tyrrhenian seas, throughout the Mediterranean and all the way to China and the Caribbean, another negative trait is visible. Over the centuries, the historical record is full of remarks about the Genoese people's tendency towards secrecy and their inconstant, moody behavior, like the winds that pushed the sails of their lucrative boats.[59]

In the main cathedral of the city, the Duomo of Genoa, an ancient inscription attributes its founding to the Roman god Janus.[60] Of course, that illustrious origin story is now dismissed as a myth, and little is known of the life of the inhabitants of the region, but in ancient times, indigenous Ligurii, who were mostly mountain dwellers, founded Genoa, most likely without realizing they were doing so. The place that became the site of the city was actually meant as a temporary meeting point for commercial activity with Phoenician and Greek merchants.[61]

The city's prehistory may seem generally uneventful, but evidence suggests that there was an active population that was engaged in significant cultural production. Archeologists have recently recovered the foundations of ancient buildings through excavations, and other digs have turned up relics, including broken statues, images and rough inscriptions. These finds suggest the remains of primitive art, and while some of it bears a resemblance to Etruscan art, other aspects of the art are distinct from developments across the Italian peninsula. This newfound archeological record suggests that there was perhaps a civilization where Genoa stands today that would date back to before the ancient Greeks began to flourish.[62]

Aside from this scant archeological record, historians do know that for a short time in the 2nd century BCE the Roman Republic annexed Liguria and connected it to a growing network of roads. Thus, in addition to being shaped by nature, it is important to acknowledge that Genoa was also influenced by the ancient Romans,[63] who called the city Genua.[64] For the Romans, Genoa represented a convenient place for stationing and deploying troops, which naturally caused the population of the city to increase.[65] Nonetheless, the impact of Roman culture appears

---

Genoese, 958-1528, xv. Throughout the history of Genoa, from the 500s through the seventeenth century, there was a strong Jewish community that lived peaceably amongst the Christian population. See Rossana Urbani and Guido Nathan Zazzu, *The Jews in Genoa: 507-1681*, vol. 2 (Leiden and Boston: BRILL Press, 1999).

[59] Gabriella Airaldi, *Genova e Liguria Nel Medioevo* (Genova: Frilli, 2007).

[60] Anonymous, *Genoa*, 2. The inscription, translated into English, reads: "Janus, the first king of Italy, and descended from the Giants, founded Genoa on this spot in the time of Abraham and Janus, Prince of Troy, skilled in astronomy, while sailing in search of a place wherein to dwell in healthfulness and security, came to the same Genoa founded by Janus, King of Italy and great-grandson (pronepos) of Noah; and seeing that the sea and the encompassing hills seemed in all things convenient, he increased it in fame and greatness." Robert Walter Carden, *The City of Genoa* (Genoa: Methuen, 1908), 1. Carden notes that excavations in 1898 uncovered a large number vases that dated all the way back to the fifth and fourth centuries BC, at last providing material confirmation for the story of Genoa's antiquity, most of which had been stolen by invaders in the intervening years. Carden, 1-2.

[61] Kirk, *Genoa and the Sea*, 5.

[62] Anonymous, *Genoa*, 1-2.

[63] Epstein, *Genoa and the Genoese, 958-1528*, 10.

[64] Anonymous, *Genoa*, 1.

[65] Anonymous, *Genoa*, 4.

to have been relatively weak, with some historians even going so far as to argue that Genoa bears the least amount of traces of Rome's dominance compared to all other Italian cities.[66] This weak influence is perhaps a testament to the strength of the cultural tradition that had already been established by its original inhabitants. It might also be a result of the fact that the Roman settlement in Genoa was relatively minor, never growing to the size of nearby Pisa.[67]

Aside from this loose connection with Rome, the historical record does not contain much detail about Genoa once the Roman Empire fell.[68] What is known is that the fall of the empire had a major impact on how Genoa was to develop because the roads that the Romans built soon fell into disrepair, which meant that it started to become more advantageous to focus on building up a fleet of ships to take on the brunt of travel.[69] The fall of Rome also meant that the surviving cities became more important, at least in relative terms.[70]

In the wake of the fall of the Roman Empire, the city of Genoa came to be controlled by several of the major powers that were active in Italy at the time and handed the city off to one another. First, the city was held by the Byzantines from 537-642, when it fell to the Lombards. They ruled the city until 774, when they were defeated by the Carolingians.[71] During this time, it was still not yet the important port or naval center it would come to be.[72]

After the death of Charlemagne, the territory passed to his son, Pepin, and histories suggest he governed the Genoese with more indulgence than his father had. This allowed the two peoples to forge a productive, peaceful relationship, after which the maritime activities of the city were able to start to grow.[73] The fall of the Carolingian dynasty ended this period of calm prosperity, but it also provided an important opening for the city as it began to take steps toward becoming a great power, with its credentials burnished by the reputation it was able to forge thanks to the relationship with the Carolingians.[74]

Nonetheless, the political shifts of power during the 9th century did little to help the growth of the city. Muslim expansion in the Mediterranean Sea resulted in constant attacks against the city in the early 930s, specifically by North Africans as the Fatimid Caliphate spread across that continent.[75] These were not confined to the Mediterranean Sea itself, but the actual city, which

---

[66] Anonymous, *Genoa*, 4.
[67] Around that time, Pisa (a central Italian city in the region of Tuscany) became an important site of trade for the Romans and a center for the production of pottery, Epstein, 5.
[68] Kirk, 5.
[69] Kirk, 6.
[70] Kirk, 6.
[71] John A. Marino and Marino Berengo, "Carolingian and Post-Carolingian Italy, 774-962," in *Encyclopedia Britannica*, accessed April 12, 2019, https://www.britannica.com/place/Italy/Carolingian-and-post-Carolingian-Italy-774-962.
[72] Kirk, 6.
[73] Anonymous, *Genoa* (London: Samuel Bentley & co, 1851), 5.
[74] Anonymous, 6.
[75] Epstein, 14.

suffered looting, murder, and one recorded account of a kidnapping of 1,000 female prisoners.[76]

In addition to the obvious human tragedy for the city, the sack of Genoa in 935 represents a substantial historiographical loss, in that the little written documentation there might have been was destroyed.[77] The Genoese people did not tend to write a great deal (as other peoples did at the time),[78] which means that the loss of the documentation in the city leaves historians with a true dearth of material. That said, Bishop Liudprand of Cremona wrote the following about the sack a few decades later: "At the same time, in the Genoese city, which has been built in the Cottian Alps, overlooking the African sea, eighty miles distant from Pavia, a spring flowed most copiously with blood, clearly suggesting to all a coming calamity. Indeed, in the same year, the Phoenicians [North Africans] arrived there with a multitude of fleets, and while the citizens were unaware, they entered the city, killing all except women and children. Then, placing all the treasures of the city and the churches of God in their ships, they returned to Africa."

Although there are virtually no records about the city from before the sack, Muslim fighters themselves wrote about the attack, and thanks to them, historians have learned that Genoa at the time was a growing town with high quality goods, such as linen thread and cloth, as well as raw silk. Thanks to these details, scholars speculate that there was active trade taking place at the time.

The one benefit for the city that emerged in the immediate aftermath is that the encounter with the Muslims worked to connect Genoa to the Mediterranean world,[79] even as the attack on the city in 935 left Genoa a mere shadow of its former self.[80] Even by 950, Genoa showed little sign that it was poised to become a dominant city in the region, but so much was to change in the coming century thanks to a resilient aristocracy in the countryside that would soon take charge of the development of the city. In fact, during the 11th century, the Genoese decided to claim their independence as a separate state, ruled under elective magistrates and consuls, and they were successful in this endeavor precisely because they had begun to show signs of becoming a formidable maritime power thanks to their relationship with the Carolingian dynasty.[81]

Although there is only secondhand material about the maritime activities of the Genoese during this post-sack period, historians do know that in the early 11th century, there were still regular attacks by Muslims against various Tyrrhenian cities, including Pisa.[82] The first documented evidence of Genoa's recovery from the sack came in 1016, the year the Genoese teamed up with

---

[76] Kirk, 7.
[77] Epstein, 14.
[78] Giovanna Petti Balbi, *Genova Medievale Vista Dai Contemporanei* (Genoa: SAGEP Editrice, 2008), 17. Balbi argues that this lack of reflective writing is a sign of the Genoese's practical nature, their rejection of contemplation without action, as well as their reserved, modest character.
[79] Kirk, 7.
[80] Epstein, 14.
[81] Anonymous, *Genoa*, 6.
[82] Kirk, 8.

the Pisans to launch a naval offensive against Muslims in Sardinia.[83] Even more dramatically, local Genoese myth also marks the year 1050 as a further sign of their renewal, because they claim they were able to capture a Muslim king in Sardinia and bring him home in triumph.[84]

What historians do know for certain is that the collaboration with Pisa was tenuous; in fact, by the 1060s, the cities of Pisa and Genoa began the first of many wars between them, likely based on a dispute surrounding the territory of nearby Sardinia.[85] However, in 1087, the two maritime cities joined forces once again to attack al-Mahdiyya, the capital of a Muslim state on the eastern coast of modern Tunisia.[86]

Genoa and the First Crusade

Around the turn of the first millennium, after their recovery from the attack, Genoese naval expansion grew at a rapid pace. Moreover, it laid the foundations for the exponential growth Genoa was to experience over the next two centuries.[87] Hand-in-hand with this investment in shipbuilding, at this time the Genoese strategy appeared to be one of aggressive anti-Muslim expansion.[88] This strategy culminated in Genoa's participation in the First Crusade (1096-1099) which is when scholars tend to mark the true inaugural moment of the Republic's history.

Following centuries of persecution, Christianity became the official religion of the Roman Empire under Constantine the Great, and the eastern half of the Empire (which later became the Byzantine Empire) took charge of Jerusalem and the Levant, controlling the area and its flow of pilgrims. But after the collapse of Rome, the Byzantines were displaced in the early 7th century by a third "Abrahamic" (after the semi-legendary founder of Judaism, Abraham) religion known as Islam, which came out of the Arabian Peninsula. An Arab Muslim army took Jerusalem in 634 A.D., and with that the Holy Land was lost to the Christians, who mourned its loss for centuries as they remained unable to take it back.

This sense of loss was exacerbated by disputes over pilgrimage rights to Jerusalem for both Christians and Jews. Since attitudes from one Muslim ruler to the next were fluid in regard to tolerance of minority religious groups, this added to a sense of uncertainty regarding Christian and Muslim access to the holy shrines, access which was paramount to ongoing Christian and Jewish identity. While it remains unclear how tolerant Muslim attitudes in the Levant during this time were over the long-term, the lack of control of such holy sites contributed to a sense of

---

[83] Epstein, 15.
[84] However, no historical evidence exists to confirm this event, Epstein, 23.
[85] Epstein, 23. In times of peace, Genoa and Pisa did also continue to work together to fend off Muslim invaders. See Walton, 13.
[86] Kirk, 8.
[87] Miner and Stantchev, 400.
[88] Mid-eleventh century, they had already reached the Egyptian city of Alexandria, and by the early twelfth century, they had established a substantial presence in Cairo—a strategy that was religiously motivated, but also no doubt aimed to disrupt Muslim shipping routes to their own benefit. Kirk, 9.

permanent anxiety among the Christians especially. Continuing patterns of expansion and contraction on the borders of the Byzantine Empire also added to the political instability of the region.

However, in the 11th century, the Arab Muslims also lost control of the Levant to a new group coming in from West Asia through Persia and Anatolia – the Seljuq Turks. After being brought in as mercenaries in 1058, they gained control of the Abassid dynasty in Baghdad, taking most of Anatolia from the failing Byzantine Empire and also conquering most of the Levant. This was part of their original purpose of fighting the new Fatimid dynasty in Egypt.

Even at its height, the Seljuq Empire lacked a strong infrastructure and existed in a state of perpetual warfare. Syria, in the Western Levant, was loosely organized into squabbling leaders distantly swearing allegiance to Baghdad and soon began to fall apart, while Palestine was contested by the Fatimids. In the wake of the empire's growing weakness, the Byzantine Emperor, Alexius Comnenus (1056-1118), saw an opportunity to regain some territory. He had hired Frankish mercenaries before, so he sent a letter to the Pope in Rome asking for more help. What was different was the Pope's reaction, which was quite startling. He called for something new – a crusade.

It is also not entirely clear how Pope Urban II came up with the idea of a crusade to the Holy Land. Gregory had made a previous call in 1074, using the term, *"milites Christi"* (soldiers of Christ), but it had been largely ignored. It is possible that Urban had heard of the Muslim concept of jihad or holy war, and the concept of aggressive expansion through holy war was not at all unknown to Christians by that period. However he conceived the idea, Urban decided to give a speech calling his audience to go on a crusade to the Holy Land, to win back Jerusalem and cleanse the Holy Land of the Muslim threat, using the Byzantine Emperor's letter as an excuse.

Urban spoke to a large number of people in Clermont, France on November 27, 1095. This was known as the Council of Clermont, and the subject was the letter from Alexius. After a brief exhortation against the fratricidal violence of the knights (Urban, himself, came from nobility), Urban related the news that the Seljuqs had conquered Romania and were attacking Europe as far west as Greece. He painted a picture of Christianity in grave danger from this new, Turkish threat, even mentioning them separately from the Arabs as another group of enemies against Christians in the Middle East.

Feudal Europe implemented what was known as the "primogeniture" system, wherein the firstborn sons automatically inherited the patriarch's titles and lands. This might have paved a solid path for the futures of the eldest sons in European families, but unless these firstborns were struck down by the plague or some other ill force of nature, this system left the second sons and so forth with no choice but to seek alternative venues for survival. Enterprising minds founded their own businesses and found other ways to make money, but many became hired guns, mercenaries, and the very first knights. These were the same men who were said to have made up the bulk of the crusaders.

Other reasons for enlistment were many and varied. Younger sons hoped to try their luck at conquering new lands and obtaining new properties overseas that they could call their own. Some seized the opportunity to broaden their horizons, and though this might have not been the ideal way to do it, sailing across the seas for an adventure was a motivation that sufficed for many. Kings rounded up rogue and ungovernable knights who needed an outlet for their bloodlust, and thereby rerouted their kleptomaniac itches towards enemy troops and villagers.

To medieval folks, salvation was measured by a figurative balance scale of sorts. One side weighed one's righteous acts, and the other, one's evil deeds; whichever side bore more weight indicated the salvation or damnation of one's soul. With that in mind, it was the Catholic mentality that all it took for a ticket to heaven was to even the score. This meant that racking up "righteous acts," including journeying on pilgrimages and obeying papal orders, could add the weight needed for the entry to Heaven. As a result, many sinners, particularly knights and warriors who had taken many a life, were some of the first to queue up for the enlistment. After all, Urban had assured them, "All who die by the way, whether by land or by sea, or in battle against the [Muslims], shall have immediate [forgiveness] of sins."

A year after Urban's famous speech, four armies of crusaders, each spearheaded by a different European power, prepped themselves to set sail for the Byzantine territories, and scheduled the date of departure for August of 1096. In an effort to seek glory for themselves, the overeager and much less experienced army of Peter the Hermit, who christened themselves the "People's Crusade," left about a month or two before the rest of the crusaders, defying the advice of Alexios himself. When Peter's army arrived at their destination, they were greeted by the far more seasoned Muslim troops, and put out of their misery in Cibotus. Soon after came the crusaders of Count Emicho, who proceeded to wreak unchecked havoc across the Jewish communities of Rhineland. To Urban's dismay, the disobedience of Emicho, which led to the slaughter of hundreds of innocent Jews, strained Christian-Jewish relations, which was not part of the plan.

The disastrous consequences of Peter and Emicho's insubordination was precisely why each of the four crusader armies were made to pledge an oath of loyalty to the pope, to which all 3, apart from Bohemond of Taranto's forces, complied. The delay proved to be worthwhile, for in May of 1097, the crusaders stormed into Nicea, the Seljuk capital of Anatolia, and had their flags planted by the end of June. One year later, the Syrian city of Antioch was theirs.

Inspired by their string of successes, the crusaders decided it was time for the main event, and headed for Jerusalem. There, they faced off with the troops of the Shi'ite Islamic caliphate, better known as the "Egyptian Fatimids." Halfway through July of 1099, the locals caved, and to the delight of the crusaders, Jerusalem was theirs once more, closing the curtains on the First

Crusade. Be that as it may, Tancred, Bohemond's nephew, had given his word to the Muslim leaders that the locals would be spared. Sadly, hundreds of innocents, including children, had fallen victim to the crusaders' swords by the end of the ordeal, which left an even fouler taste in Muslim mouths.

Medieval depiction of the Siege of Jerusalem

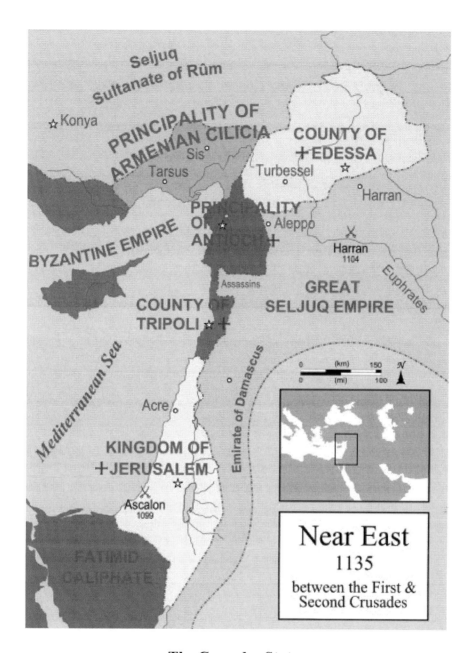

The Crusader States

Contrary to modern Muslim views of the Crusades, contemporary Islam was not especially traumatized or disrupted by the Crusades. The First Crusade in particular had little effect on the Muslim chroniclers, and the Muslim response is found scattered through various histories of what their writers considered greater concerns.

There were various reasons for this. First, Palestine existed in a contested area between the Abbasid Seljuq Empire of Baghdad in what is now Iraq and the Fatimid Empire in Egypt, based in Cairo. The contemporary and even later Muslim sources seemed to be confused about the origins and intent of the Crusaders. Further, both empires were not cohesive entities but squabbling groups of city rulers that existed in a fragile and constantly shifting set of alliances and rivalries. There was very little consistency of Muslim loyalty or alliance and no Pan-Arab, let alone Pan-Muslim, identity. Ibn Al-Athir, for example, believed that the Franks had been hired as mercenaries by the Fatimids against the Abbasids, not by the Byzantines to reclaim Byzantine territory. The religious motive of crusade was largely ignored.

Another important reason the First Crusade was probably downplayed by Muslim writers was the fact that the chroniclers were mostly Arabs, but most of the armies that the Crusaders fought were Turkish armies fighting for Turkish interests. The Seljuqs had recently displaced the Arab elites, so there was a disconnect between the damage the Crusaders were doing to individual rulers and the concerns of the writers recording the events. Unlike the Frankish, or even the Byzantine source of Anna Comnena, the Arab historians felt little personal involvement in the events surrounding the crusade and thus did not ascribe great importance to it.

Lastly, and perhaps most importantly, the Crusaders did not threaten the actual centers of Muslim power by passing through and claiming the contested territory of Palestine and western Syria. The distant power centers of Baghdad and Cairo were never touched or threatened, so the Crusaders were not considered a great threat by either the Abbasid Sultan or the Fatimid Caliph. This attitude would change, but not for several decades.

Meanwhile, as they were still riding the high of a victory that came much sooner than expected, many of the crusaders made the journey back home. A fraction was left behind to manage the newly conquered territories, which they called "Crusader States," or by its alternative moniker, the "Outremer," a take on the French translation of "overseas." The Crusader States consisted of dominions in Jerusalem, Antioch, Tripoli, and Edessa, where new Christian-governed castles and fortifications would rise from the ashes. Their rule was uninterrupted for about 45 years, until Zangi, the general of Mosul, and his men broke through the borders of Edessa unannounced and seized the state in 1144.

The legacy of the First Crusade was wide reaching, and thanks to the success, the Genoese trading routes and practices began to evolve.[89] Whereas Genoese ships had not visited the East with any regularity before the First Crusade,[90] after contributing this important military power to the Christian war, many Genoese decided to remain in the Holy Land afterwards with an eye towards setting up trading colonies.[91] If this dual identity as crusaders and traders sounds unusual, it was not, as these soldiers-turned-merchants shared a double role with counterparts from Venice, Pisa, and even Catalonia. However, it was an identity unique to the Mediterranean in the Middle Ages, a time of unprecedented fluidity in which travelers were able to occupy the roles of businessmen, crusaders, merchants, and diplomats. They played crucial roles in the political and economic spheres of the region. Moreover, these Genoese crusaders had the

---

[89] "During this time, the Genoese traded typical products of the Mediterranean, including salt, timber, cheese, wine, grains and olive oil," Miner and Stantchev, 400.
[90] Miner and Stantchev, 400.
[91] Walton, xi.

opportunity to negotiate the porous boundaries between different cultures and religious groups, including Eastern and Western Christians, as well as Muslims and Jews.[92]

Once they were entrenched in the politics and economics of the Holy Land, these hybrid soldier-merchants quickly moved in to provide maritime defense as well as transportation between the Holy Land and the core Christian areas of Europe. Indeed, providing these services earned the Genoese legal protections and other advantages over other merchants who attempted to gain a foothold in the east. The commerce in the east after the First Crusade provided Genoa's economy with a quick infusion of money that was then immediately reinvested in further commercial activity.[93]

Not all crusaders remained in the Holy Land. Many of those who returned to Liguria brought relics back with them, including the reputed remains of John the Baptist, and later expeditions brought home what was thought to be the Holy Grail used by Christ at the Last Supper.[94] Thanks to the First Crusade and this abundance of relics and booty, Genoa was transformed from a small port city to a truly formidable naval power. The crusaders also brought back valuable commodities such as pepper, suggesting that trading that would soon be happening with the East. Finally, Genoa earned itself more territories, including piazzas in the Holy City and Jaffa, with a promise for more if they participated in future conquests.[95]

The Start of an Empire

As Venice approached the 9th century, the community had begun to make a ripple – however small – in the waters. Nestled in the kernel of the lagoon on the coast of northeastern Italy, right along the shore of the Adriatic Sea, which was the crystal-blue body of water sandwiched between Italy and the coasts of Slovenia to Greece, the city's location made it a premier spot for lucrative trading opportunities. In time, Venice would play a key role in building trade routes that linked Europe to eastern trading ports.

---

[92] Merv Mack, "Genoa and The Crusades." In *A Companion to Medieval Genoa*, edited by Carrie E. Benes. (Leiden and Boston: BRILL Press, 2018) 471.
[93] Miner and Stantchev, 400.
[94] Walton, 14.
[95] Walton, 15.

A map of the Republic of Venice in 1000

With its proximity to these eastern ports, as well as the traders in the Byzantine Empire, the growing city became a middleman. The city received shipments of exotic goods from Asia and the Middle East, then distributed the cargo to various cities across western Europe for a sweet profit. The exclusive trading rights to the entirety of the Adriatic Coast granted to Venice by the Byzantine Empire gave them a monopoly of sorts on eastern imports. And so, this leg-up in the race allowed them to thrive in what would have otherwise been a crushingly competitive market.

Products from what was known as the "Orient" were particular favorites of the Europeans. Oriental goods tended to be associated with the cream of the crop in society, consisting of high quality items such as silk, precious stones, stellar gems, and an assortment of medicinal and cooking spices and herbs. The less glamorous, but equally essential commodities such as wood, iron, tin, copper, and other metals were transported across Europe via land-based trading routes.

However, the golden geese of the Venetian trade lay not with oriental luxuries, but with food-related items. Venetians had signed trading agreements with other Italian cities that designated them as the sole supplier of salt to the mainland. In addition to the vast quantities of salt they produced locally, they sniffed out the salt reserves across Europe and purchased as much as they could where they could find them, in places such as Sicily, Sardinia, Libya, Cyprus, and the Balearic Islands.

The profits raked in from their control of the Adriatic salt trade gave them the freedom to test out the market and break into new business opportunities. As the historian S.A. Adshead put it, "For the Venetians, salt was not a commodity among commodities…it greased the wheels of all the working parts and fueled its motor." Eventually, the Venetians homed in on the wheat trade.

In later centuries, barley, rye, oats, millet, and cereal became imperative when it came to feeding the swiftly multiplying inhabitants of the city. Venetian authorities took it upon themselves to oversee all wheat-related sea trade for both quality and quantity, as well as price control. Later, Venice would also dabble in the trades of wine, oil, and cane sugar.

Though there was already an abundance of wine and oil in Venice, the local merchants purchased these goods from other Italian cities or Mediterranean countries, anyway. Some merchants sold the imported wine and oil to those who could afford it in Venice for a mark-up. Others repackaged the imports and resold them to their clients overseas.

As Venice found its footing in international trade, it had to deal with the geopolitics surrounding it, and despite its famous moniker, early Venice was by no means "serene." Following the founding of Venice came decades of internal political struggle as the Venetians disagreed amongst themselves about how to handle ties with Byzantine authorities. In the early 9th century, in fact, a pair of brothers who served as Doge joined up with the Bishop of nearby Zara, and by tentatively allying themselves with the Holy Roman Emperor Charlemagne, for the first time in their history they staged an open rebellion against the Byzantines. This bought them a small amount of autonomy, but it also meant Venice was now caught between two powerful empires. The city needed to maintain a difficult balance in order to preserve autonomy, and even after some of its leaders worked with Charlemagne, Venetians at one point sought help from the Byzantines to keep Charlemagne from seizing too much control of their territory.

Thanks to savvy negotiations, Venice was able to strike a balance and benefit from its proximity to the two empires, at least insofar as the superpowers helped the city retain its independence from the Italian mainland. When the Lombard kingdom was absorbed by the Franks, Venice was able to reaffirm its connection to the Byzantine Empire.

A crucial moment came when Charlemagne and the Byzantine emperor went to war with one another, and Venice was able to reap the rewards of the peace treaty. The Pax Nicephori of 803 explicitly declared the Venetian dukedom to be a part of the Byzantine Empire, and Charlemagne, already in declining health, accepted the unfavorable terms without further fight. However, the Byzantine empire also suffered some losses in signing the treaty, so Venice was one of the few winners, gaining all of the political, cultural, and commercial benefits of the peace without losing its independence. The Venetians were technically still Byzantine citizens who all had Byzantine honorifics and funding, but following the Pax Nicephori, they began to perceive themselves as Venetians, and they felt beholden to the fellow Venetians who elected them into power. Indeed, after the Pax Nicephori, the Byzantine Empire never again seriously interfered with their politics, and as the Byzantines got caught up dealing with closer enemies in the east, the Venetians explicitly refused to accept a subordinate position to any of the Germanic tribal kings who still held any power in Europe.

Another major benefit of the city's position between the two empires is that they were able to avoid falling into the feudal system that was a common practice in Lombardy and Tuscany. Instead, they were able to develop their own form of mixed government that served them well, and they avoided falling into the seemingly endless wars of Guelf against Ghibelline that continued on and off throughout the peninsula for years and caused substantial economic setbacks to those involved. For the remainder of the 9th century, the Republic was on a major upwards swing.

In fact, by being independent but being in the middle of everything, the Republic of Venice was able to acquire an ideal position by playing the role of intermediary, both in terms of politics and commerce. Furthermore, in addition to being the main middleman of international sea trade, Venice was also a major exporter of timber and glass, and by the 13th century, glass manufacturing had become another of the city's major industries. The artisans behind the glass-making wizardry were respected members of society, their offspring often marrying into the richest of the rich in the community. Glass artisans were urged to keep their unique glass-making techniques within their families. Keeping the secrets of various trades within the borders only added another edge to the rising power of Venice.

A traveler arriving in Venice during this time in the High Middle Ages would have found a dense concentration of buildings, houses and palaces, stores and churches, all towering above its watery horizon, yet in surprising harmony. At the time, it was a remarkably urban city, where houses, streets, stones and people were far more common than the grass and the trees that would have dominated other contemporary cities. Venetians tended to agree with this characterization, and they were particularly proud of their unique connection to the environment, which featured prominently in artistic representations of the time. This pride in the lagoon, of course, was matched with a certain humility, as the Venetians recognized that their geographic location would be both their greatest challenge and, potentially, their most prized resource.

While the Venetians are constantly associated with the Mediterranean, during the Middle Ages they were better known as able boatsmen who could navigate the local rivers, and there are surviving records in which their leaders attempted to negotiate commercial treatises for them in order to protect them from the dangers they found on the rivers of the Po Valley. Following the Pax Nicefori, political conditions started to become more stable in the Po Valley, and the population grew rapidly and cities multiplied in size. This increased the demand for luxury goods from the east, and it also meant that there were more goods being produced for export. Driven by the opportunity for profit, the Venetian people started to turn their efforts away from the rivers and instead head out to sea.

The Venetians quickly experienced the first fruits of their maritime prosperity, boosted somewhat ironically by their former ties with the Byzantines, which provided important trade markets for them. The lumber trade and Venice's production of iron and hemp (all materials that stimulated their shipbuilding prowess) allowed the Venetians to further spur on the development of their empire. The Venetian people were also actively involved in the slave trade, trafficking slaves east and acquiring vast quantities of precious metals in exchange, and thanks to their political association with the Byzantine Empire, Venice was able to take control of the European spice trade, serving as the port of entry for the West. If that was not enough, its easy accessibility to the Germanic center of Europe made Venice a market for mineral wealth, including silver, copper, iron and other metals.

As the Venetians' commercial activities grew unabated, they continued to participate politically in the shifting global scene. Although their activities before 1000 are relatively obscure, it is known that the Venetians scored a series of naval victories and began to establish military control of the upper Adriatic around that time. Less than a century later, Venice was fighting for control of the lower Adriatic along the coast of Albania.

As they improved in military strength, they remained selective about choosing which external conflicts to fight in, which was certainly one reason for the empire's longstanding success. Starting around 1075, when the Italian peninsula was plagued by conflict between the papacy and nearby powers, Venice asserted its neutrality. For example, during the First Crusade at the end of the 11th century, Venice participated but chose not to help capture Jerusalem, whereas Pisa and Genova did. Instead, Venice saved its strength, and after the Crusaders took the Holy City, the Venetians sought trading opportunities in Jerusalem after the fighting ended.

As the riches from all the new ventures rained down upon Venice, the city's confidence began to swell, and the succeeding doges continued on the mission to refine the community's defenses. One of the most important but least understood figures was Ordelafo Faliero, the 34th Doge of Venice, son of Vitale Faliero de' Doni, the 32nd doge. Time can once again be blamed for the scarcity of information that has survived regarding the doge and his background. Apart from Faliero's prior membership in the Minor Council – an assembly of "apostolic families" that served as judges, ambassadors, and other posts of the like – the only other confirmed detail of his personal life was his marriage to Matelda Faliero, a relative of King Baldwin I of Jerusalem.

A medieval depiction of Ordelafo Faliero

The doges who preceded him had already planted flags and claimed a third of the lands in Mira, Jaffa, and Rhodes, securing free trade agreements with each conquered territory. When Faliero was elected to the post in 1102, he was determined to continue his predecessors' policy of territorial and commercial expansion in the Holy Land. Just a few months into his reign, Faliero was given the chance to sharpen his combat techniques and subjugation skills by assisting the King of Jerusalem in the capture of Syria. Bolstered by the smooth seizure of the territory, Faliero and his men went on to conquer Dalmatia, Croatia, and other small provinces.

Faliero was eventually bested by the Hungarian forces in 1117 during a skirmish in Zadar, Croatia, but his hunger for expansion is not the reason his name has been bolded in Italian history books. Instead, it was his construction of the so-called "nucleus" of the Venetian Arsenal. The doge was among the first to look beyond the mountainous obstacles that came attached with start-up societies, and saw the true potential of the budding republic. Venice was about to take the world by storm – he was certain of it.

In 1104, Doge Ordelafo Faliero began construction of a shipyard known as the "Arsenale Vecchio," which was derived from an Arabic term meaning "place of manufacture." It began as a side project of the state, its purpose to maintain a modest stream of additional income by serving as the main manufacturer and repair station for local commercial fleet, as well as the ships of its own naval forces.

The reinforcement of defenses was particularly critical at this time, as throughout the 11th and 12th centuries, Venice found itself repeatedly harassed by lawless pirates looking to either capture Venetian ships and make an easy payday off the cargo, or tamper with trading posts on the Dalmatian coast and other Venetian-owned strongholds. The doges sent one Venetian fleet after another to quell these attacks. Needless to say, the Venetian fleets and city security had to be kept in tip-top shape.

Meanwhile, more trouble was brewing. The sovereigns of the Byzantine Empire began to regret the exclusive trading rights they had signed over to the Venetians, and found the city's newfound prosperity difficult to swallow. In an effort to counter the Venetians' rising fortunes, Byzantine leaders established new trading agreements with Genoa and Pisa in 1169 and the year after, respectively. In 1171, Byzantine authorities demanded the confiscation of all goods and commodities in an effort to target every last one of the Venetian merchants in the empire.

Though the Byzantine leaders had attempted to hit the Venetians where it hurt, the city chose to remain on the sidelines for the remaining part of the century, allowing the empire to come to its own undoing. It was here that the Venetians displayed not just the capability to protect themselves, but the daring and cunning that would keep them at the peak for centuries to come. In 1195, the Byzantine emperor, Isaac II, was booted from the throne and blinded in an attack by his own blood brother. The emperor's son, Alexius, was nabbed and jailed until he finally escaped in 1201, seeking refuge in Western Europe.

That same year, plans for the Fourth Crusade in the Middle East, engineered by Pope Innocent III and Western European forces, were in the works. This time, the starting point of the crusaders was to be set in Venice. From Venice, the crusaders would sail to Egypt, which was believed to have been the weakest link of Sultan Saladin of the Ayyubid Dynasty's Middle Eastern empire. The Venetians cooked up an offer the crusaders found difficult to refuse. They promised to provide a grand supply of support – enough vessels to house 20,000 foot soldiers, 4,500 knights, their horses, and 9,000 squires (chivalrous page boys). 50 Venetian galleys would be sent along with them for added protection. As another bonus, the crusaders would be given ships stocked with enough food to last them a year, which was the estimated length of the mission. In return, the crusaders would foot the bill of 85,000 silver marks, as well as an equal portion of the new lands the crusaders conquered. With the terms of the agreement aligned, a departure date was set for June of 1202.

Unbeknownst to the crusaders, Venetian diplomats had also stealthily reached out to the Egyptian sultan himself. They informed him of the impending invasion, but assured him they had no intentions of allowing the crusaders to reach their intended destination. At the same time, Venetian agents were in talks with the son of the disgraced Byzantine emperor, and relayed their grievances with the tumultuous empire.

By the summer of 1202, the crusaders had pieced together their forces but had failed to come up with the 85,000 marks. It appeared as if the Venetians had been expecting this, for they had a compromise waiting at hand. They would accept a delay in payment if the crusaders made a pit stop at Zara in Dalmatia, where they would reclaim the city on behalf of the Venetians, thereby snatching the territory from the Hungarian king's hands. The crusaders agreed, and set sail for Zara on November 8, arriving 2 days later. By the end of the 8-day siege, it was no longer safe to continue on their eastbound journey. They had no choice but to set up a winter camp in Zara, sitting on their hands as they waited for the thaw of winter.

With the crusaders stranded in Zara, the Venetians contacted Alexius once more, where both parties came to another side agreement. If the Venetians could somehow find a way to secure the Byzantine throne for Alexius, he would not only relieve the crusaders of their debt with the Venetians, but supply manpower, weapons, and whatever financial support they needed. The crusaders were none too happy by the change of plans, but they grudgingly accepted.

In June of 1203, the crusaders arrived in Constantinople and carried through with their end of the deal. With Alexius IV seated at the throne, he set out to repay the Venetians by swiping church property and fattening the tax rates. Unsurprisingly, morale plummeted, along with his approval ratings among the citizens of Constantinople. Meanwhile, the crusaders, who were still stationed just outside of Constantinople, were also growing restless. In April of 1204, Venetian agents swooped in and paid another visit to the crusaders, coaxing them into entering Constantinople once more and replacing Alexius with a Latin emperor.

Following what is now referred to as the "1204 Sack of Constantinople," Venice finally gained the independence it had so desperately yearned for. Rather than torch the place to the ground, the Venetians looted the Byzantine establishments and brought the booty, including the prized bronze horses of St Mark's Cathedral, back home. With that, the Republic of Venice solidified its status once more as the central trading hub of the West, and even better yet, they now had jurisdiction over the territories and the trading routes of Crete and Euboea. The maritime territories of Venice's overseas empire was collectively christened the "Stato da Màr," or "Domini da Mar," which translates to "state or domains of the sea." Other than the islands of Crete and Euboea, lands under Venetian authority included Albania, Dalmatia, Istria,

Negroponte, Cyprus, the Kingdom of Morea, and other Aegean islands.

With the Stato da Màr set in place, Venetians now had full access to eastern Mediterranean trade. It also provided them with a much sturdier shield that protected them against foreign intruders and maritime rivals. In conjunction with that, the Byzantine trading agreements with the Pisans and the Genoese expired, driving their biggest opponents out of the competition.

Even so, the Venetians knew this was no time for complacency. Much more work lay ahead if they wanted to hold on to their expanding power.

While the Venetian Arsenal was said to have originated some time in the 12th century, the first known mention of the shipyard on paper would only come a century later. According to the antique file, the arsenal at the time consisted of a pair of squeri, the Italian term for "boatyards," that were built along a dock connected to the San Marco basin. A series of "crenelated," or walls topped with equally spaced rectangular notches, lined the site. By the time Dante mentioned it in his legendary work, the arsenal was home to caches of naval tools and provisions, repair shops, a secured base that served as the Venetian maritime headquarters, and a small armory. And the Venetians were only getting started.

The first Venetian squeri were small establishments run by boat craftsmen known as "squerarioli." Each squeri handled the manufacturing of one type of boat, which aided greatly in speeding up the production process. When a new vessel was completed, the finished product would be pushed down a sloped apparatus resembling an open chute, and slid into the nearest canal.

Venetian squerarioli went on to develop different types of vessels to suit the needs of their clients. First, there was the galley, a warship most recognizable for its long, slender body and its rows of oars, manned by dozens of men on 2 lower decks. The first galleys navigated the seas with the help of only a single square sail, but later models sported "lateen" sails, which were triangular pieces added to the mast at an angle. Venetian galleys were one of the classic medieval battleships, as it was one of the elementary vessels to maneuver, and its narrow beam made it easy to board enemy ships as well.

An 18th century painting of the Venetian navy

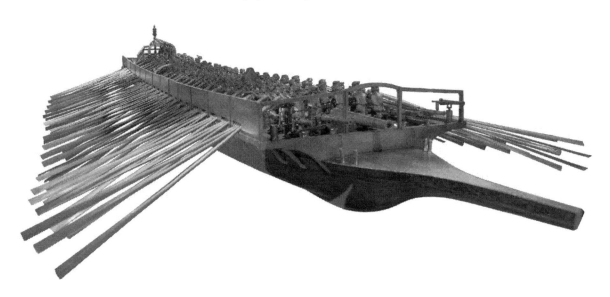

A model of a Venetian galley

The cog was a merchant ship reminiscent of a medieval round ship, preferred by traders for their speed, reliability, and ability to transport high volumes of cargo. Cogs had wider beams and rounded edges (otherwise known as the "bow and stern"). The first models used square sails, but these were later substituted with 2 smaller masts placed in the front and the rear of the vessel.

This boat became such a hot commodity that by the 14th century, Denmark invested in replacing a fleet of 1,000 dated longships with gleaming cogs.

Around this time, another vessel would be developed in Venice – possibly the most renowned of them all. Today, this boat most likely springs up in the eye of one's mind whenever the city is touched upon as a subject of discussion, complete with a handsome, crooning man in a striped shirt, the red ribbons on his straw hat flapping in the wind. This, of course, is the gondola, which has been around as early as the 11th century, but unlike the light, curved body of the sleek, streamlined version seen today, the 13th century gondola was much bulkier, and required 12 oars. 2 centuries later, gondolas had shed off the extra inches on their hips, but they had acquired a cabin, known as a "felze." By the 16th century, the boats had become so over-engineered and smothered with cumbersome decorations that Venetian authorities were compelled to take action, ordering for the dialing down of aesthetic treatments on all gondolas. On a related note, a sister to the gondola was the sandolo, which was a 2-seater, flat-bottomed rowing boat made especially for the shallow waters in the city.

Saffron Blaze's picture of gondolas in Venice

In 1225, the first extension to the Arsenale Vecchio, or in English, the "Old Armory," was built, which focused on the construction of a new dock, more buildings, and manufacturing plants towards the eastern belt of the premises. The construction of this new addition would last until the beginning of the 14th century, and was launched as the "Darsena Grande," approximately 8.7 hectares in size, no minor feat for the time.

Jean-Pierre Dalbéra's picture of the Old Arsenal

In 1312, Dante Alighieri, along with Guido Novello da Polenta, the mayor of Ravenna, a northern Italian city, came to Venice. As was customary with the most eminent guests, the dignified duo was escorted around the arsenal campus. The 3 houses where Dante and Polenta lodged, as well as each of their bridges, were later renamed the Palazzos of Inferno, Paradiso, and Purgatorio (Hell, Paradise, and Purgatory) as a personal nod to Dante's literary masterpiece. These buildings were later revamped in the 15th century.

By the end of the 13th century, shipbuilding was no longer just a side project but a solid enterprise, raking in sterling profits for the state. Starting from the 1290s, the doges authorized the funding and assemblage of warships that accompanied merchant galleys during their travels to the ports of Romania, Alexandria, and the Levant for additional cargo security. It did not take much effort to round up the men needed for the new arrangement, as most Venetian sailors were trained fighters. Reputable members of merchant families also tagged along as "gentlemen of the quarterdeck," sharing various responsibilities in voyage management. Veterans of these posts were later bumped up to the titles of captain or admiral.

The presence of the warships proved worthwhile. In the 1300s, Venetian convoys tackled the

Genoese trading routes via the English Channel and the coasts of the North Sea, allowing them access to the recently-formed Hanseatic League, which was a network of merchant guilds situated predominantly in northern Europe. Things were all falling neatly into place.

In 1304, the arsenal introduced its first rope factory on the southern end of the arsenal. Designed by Antonio da Ponte, the Corderie della Tana, or Casa del Canevo, opened its doors 18 years later. It was a grand establishment for its day, with 2 stories and a roof erected by strong wooden trusses, measuring 316 meters in length and about 9.70 meters tall. The interior was split into 3 naves and 2 mezzanine floors, which were low-story "intermediate" floors wedged between the ceiling and the ground, mostly found in industrial warehouses. The Corderie harbored heaps of hemp, which was used to produce cables and ropes of different lengths, widths, and textures for ships.

In 1311, Venetian craftsmen presented the majestic *Bucintoro*, a glinting galley coated in gold that bore a striking statue of Lady Justice. The *Bucintoro*, or in English, the "*Bucentaur*," was an ornately embellished pleasure barge, which were flat-bottomed, snail-paced boats used for leisure or ceremonial purposes. The double-decker bucentaur in question featured a canopy, or "tiemo," separated in 2 parts. One was decorated in red velvet for Venetian nobles, and the other decked out in royal purple, which was reserved for the doge.

On the 17th of August that year, it was announced that a new stipulation would be added to the Promissione Ducale, which was the oath all doges were to take when they were sworn in. The provision stated "that a Bucentaur should be made for the Lord Doge for his rule, and it should be held in the Arsenale." From then on, the Venetian state would finance the construction of all future bucentaurs with public funds.

A new tradition unfolded. Starting from 1311, the ducal bucentaur was to be used in the annual "Sposalizio del Mare," or "Marriage of the Sea" ceremony, which took place every Ascension Day. This was a commemoration that represented the "maritime supremacy of Venice," involving a grim procession of boats with the bucentaur in the lead. Out at sea, the doge twisted the blessed gold ring his off finger and flung it into the water as he declared, "Desponsamus te, mare," or in English, "We wed thee, sea!" The bucentaur would later be used for other state ceremonies, such as festivals that honored the Virgin Mother, as well as to transport the doges' freshly-crowned wives, known to the Venetians as the "dogaressas," to the palace.

An 18th century painting depicting a bucentaur on Ascension Day

In the meantime, another addition had been added to the arsenal, as more ships (25 galleys at least) and equipment were needed for the renewed conflict with Genoa. This extension, the Arsenale Nuovo, or the "New Arsenal," was built between 1303 and 1325. Large plots of wetlands, along with the San Daniele Lake to the east of the Vecchio, had to be purchased to make room for the expansion.

A picture of the towers at the entrance to the arsenal

The establishment of the Nuovo had been a wise decision. Whereas the Vecchio could handle the production of only 40 galleys each year, the Nuovo could pump out 80 with no problem. Factories were also erected in the southern part of the arsenal to handle the production of oars, anchors, cables, chains, tar, and rigging systems. This cluster of manufacturing plants became known as the "Campagna."

The Arsenale would have been nothing if it were not for the faceless heroes behind the operation – the Arsenalotti, the community behind what was supposedly the "largest industrial complex in all of Europe." Behind the walls, the Arsenalotti had developed a society of their own. The profound backbone of their well-organized hierarchical structure earned them the respect of not just the Venetian locals, but snagged the attention of ducal eyes, too. On top of manufacturing ships and equipment for the state, these members were held with such high regard that they were entrusted with some of the most desired duties, such as the steering of the *Bucintoro*. To the doges, the Arsenalotti was a second family, privy to the most confidential of state secrets. They were present at all the meetings held by the Grand Council in the Doge's Palace, not merely as flies on the wall, but to "guard the guards," and also handled the security during doge funerals. What was more, the higher-ups of the Arsenalotti managed the fire brigade and governed the "zecca," their state coin.

Apart from the prestige tied to those within the organization, there were plenty of inviting incentives to being a member of the Arsenalotti. They were rewarded with lavish salaries, free living quarters for their families and future descendants, and other attractive benefits. Word spread of the industrial nirvana, reeling in talents from all over Europe and across the seas. Soon, it had become a bustling community of caulkers, marangoni (Arsenale carpenters), oarsmen, turners, sawyers, blacksmiths, rope makers, and other laborers.

The secrets of the craft were locked away and only those in the Arsenalotti had the keys, which were to be passed down generation after generation. As well taken care of as they were, the state expected absolute loyalty from them; what the state gave, it could just as easily take away. Those who stole, misappropriated funds, or tainted their words risked the wrath of the state, and were made to face either exile, or in some cases, even death.

Knowing disloyalty would be inevitable at some point, the state took extra care in policing those at the Arsenalotti. Later on, for instance, to prevent theft, every tool, down to each nail that was used in the Arsenalotti, bore a small carving of a winged lion. The winged lion was the symbol of Venice, which was chosen to honor the city's patron saint, Mark the Evangelist. Oral tradition dictated that Mark had graced the Venetian lagoon with his presence. There, he was greeted by an angel, which bore life-changing tidings: "May peace be with you, Mark...Here, your body will rest."

Dedication was required to climb up the ladder of the Arsenalotti. Following an apprenticeship period of about 6 or 7 years, apprentices were promoted to the title of "mastro," or "master." The experts of the craft were the "proti," or "director of works," and were in charge of vessel designing and the manufacturing process, as well as supervising the order of operations of oarsmen, marangoni, caulkers, and other related fields.

A proti could aspire to be an Appontadore, or "timer," who kept track of the time and progress of the project, managed quality control, and disciplined those who were absent or habitually late. A Stimadore (assessor) was tasked with the inspection of finished products and drawing up reports of individual work performances. The questionnaires they filled usually involved the following matters – a ranking of their skills, their attendance records, whether or not they complied with rules and obeyed their superiors, how well they educated their underlings, and so forth. In the same breath, some of the questions were queerly personal, including whether or not the worker used profanities in the workplace, and if they were "quiet, or grumblers." The stimadore was also placed in charge of the community's timber usage, the marangoni, and setting the working hours for each given field in the business.

A council of the most esteemed proti in the Arsenalotti came to fruition in 1276, branding themselves the "protomastri." There was a trio of Patroni, each to hold their posts for no more than 32 months. These were not just lawmakers or supervisors, but were also the peacemakers of the tight ship that they run.

The Patron in Guardia was responsible for regulating and administering all the warehouses in the Palazzo of Inferno. They were the only ones among the proti who were not allowed at the Grand Council meetings, for they were required to remain at their posts all day. They were also expected to check in with the guards of the Arsenalotti at least once daily.

The Patron Casser signed off on and double-checked all incoming orders and outgoing shipments, and held dominion over the Palazzo of Purgatory. Cassers also monitored each vessel for any faults or imperfections vigilantly, and ensured that each ship underwent head-to-toe checkups every 3 days. Every 3 months, they filed progress reports and shared commentaries with their counterparts in the council. Additionally, each supply of ships, sails, ropes, ammunition, and other equipment had to be thoroughly counted and recorded. A minimum of 20 galleys was to be armed and ready at all times.

Finally, the Patron in Banca headed the Palazzo of Paradise, and acted as the department of finance for the Arsenalotti. All crunched numbers and financial logs were neatly stored in a "main book" dubbed the "giornalieri." At the end of each year, the other 2 patrons compared notes with the logs kept by the Banca to check for any inconsistencies.

Sitting at the top of the chain was the "ammiraglio," the "admiral" or "supreme commander" of the Arsenalotti in general. He was responsible for the "total quality" of procedures and finalized products in the arsenal. The ammiraglio was elected by the protomastri, and unlike the other positions, had no term limits. Directly under the ammiraglio was his right-hand man, the capitano, who maintained the discipline among the community and acted as the assertive hand if the situation called for it. Then, there was the gastaldo, the recruiter of new craftsmen. Assistants-for-hire that were paid by the day were known as the "bastasi" or "facchini."

The working hours of the Arsenalotti were fairly reasonable for its time, and varied depending on the season. In the early months of the year, craftsmen clocked in at 10:30 in the morning and worked until 1:30 in the afternoon. They were given a 1.5 hour rest break before work resumed at 3, and later called it a day at half past 5. From July-December, working hours doubled, but remained within the 9-hour limit, starting from 3:00 to 9:30, then again at 4 in the afternoon to 6:30 in the evening. Elderly craftsmen, women, and children were given an extra half-hour off each day, whereas masters were given an hour more. In the late 15th century, children would be banned from the workforce altogether.

It was only towards the 14th century that the Arsenale decided to dip their toes into weapon and ammunition production. To ease the new field of production into their routine, it was agreed that they would play it safe, and start small. The first weapons produced in Venice were standard weapons that had been around for years, such as axes, spears, swords, and crossbows. Early

Venetians were especially comfortable with the last on the list, and as of 1303, were required by law to have undergone basic crossbow training. When "proper firearms" picked up in popularity centuries later, authorities restricted use of these complex, volatile, and "unwieldy" weapons to the Venetian army.

In the 1370s, Venetian craftsmen introduced an improved version of the medieval bombard, which were archaic cannons that expelled balls of stone or steel. From then on, all local naval fleets were outfitted with bombards. A fraction of the arsenal's craftsmen were also assigned to build early models of guns to be used in the Genoese conflicts later on.

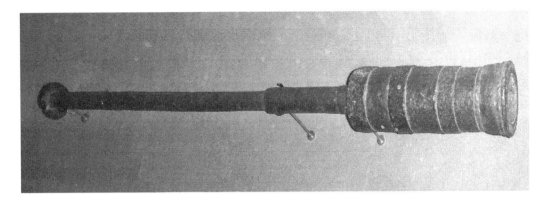

A 14th century bombard

A 15th century bombard

Be that as it may, it was said that for the first half of the 1400s, the enthusiasm and interest expressed for these novel weapons remained flickering to dim at best. There was much resistance to change, and for good reason. The first firearms were horribly flawed – they often missed their targets, and were excruciatingly slow to reload. The success rate was abysmal, and they worked once in battle – if they worked at all. Even so, the Venetian army saw a spark within the new weapons that others chose to disregard. They stuck to their guns, and continued to use them in battle – once in the 1426 Siege of Brescia, as well as the attack on Milanese camps based in Caravaggio. To remedy the deficiencies of these firearms, the arsenal craftsmen worked to conjure up ways to improve or better incorporate guns to their weapons.

One example of their genius was the mace-gun combination, which was exactly how it sounds. Built into the center of a flanged mace was the concealed barrel of a gun. This came in handy as a kind of Hail Mary; the simple light of a fuse on the spherical end of the handle prompted the weapon to fire. It was later upgraded to spew 4 bullets at a time. Other clever contraptions conceived were sword guns, hatchet guns, and the father of the modern revolver. A man named Bartolomeo Colleoni was said to have been the first to install firearms and cannons on carriages, an ancestor of the armored tank.

Although Venetians were more intrigued than they were convinced about transitioning to firearms at this point, their progress in the field had not gone unnoticed. In 1436, a highly-regarded goldsmith from the city of Ulm, known only as "Master John," was granted permission from the German government for a 2-year stay in Venice, which he spent poring over the Venetians' firearms and weapons technology – in particular, their multipurpose capabilities. This was certainly not something to dismiss, as the Germans were considered the forerunners in the world of artillery at the time.

In the latter half of the 15th century, the importance of expanding upon and modernizing artillery technology finally registered with the Venetians. Gunners and cannon-makers were hired, and foundries propped up in droves. Demand exceeded capacity in 1463 when Maestro Francesco was commissioned to produce 6 bombards at one time. Not only were their facilities unable to keep up with production, one of the bombards ordered was so big, not a furnace in the city could host the enormous cannon.

A Bosnian gunfounder (one who operates a gun foundry) and bombard specialist, Bartolemeo da Cremona, is the individual credited with the transformation of artillery organization. One of his most celebrated achievements was his men's speedy manufacturing of guns used in the Turkish War, as well as the Siege of Trieste, a city/seaport in the northern neck of the country. His salary amounted to about 100 ducats a year (roughly $25,000 USD today), and he proceeded to serve as chief gunfounder for over 2 decades. Cremona was later replaced by a native, Sigismondo Alberghetti, who received double the salary, making 200 ducats annually ($50,000). Alberghetti would be the last Italian to hold the post for a time. Likewise, most of the gunners in

Venice at this point were immigrants. As these talents were mostly sought out, these foreigners typically earned more than the average Venetian, earning about 15 ducats a month, which was triple the locals' salary.

The artillery section of the Venetian Arsenal was advancing swimmingly. As told by one of its visitors in his diary, English writer John Evelyn, the brilliant armory was a place rich with "cannon, bullets, chains, grapples, grenadoes...and over that arms for 800,000 men...together with weapons of offense and defense for 62 ships." Another visitor, an English soldier who served in the English Civil War, echoed Evelyn's awe. He had seen "arms in 2 rooms for 3,000 horses...arms for 10,000 horses in another room; and in another, arms for 50 galleys." The rooms that housed the valuable ammunition were labeled the "Garden of Oranges."

In the 15th century, the Arsenal was considered the "world's largest industrial complex," boasting more than 3,000 members within its community. By 1410, the Venetian Navy was the proud owner of at least 3,300 post-primed warships, courtesy of the Arsenale, fueled by a force of 36,000 sailors. They showed no signs of slowing down any time soon.

Genoa and the Late Middle Ages

During the almost three centuries between the First Crusade and the War of Chioggia against Venice from 1378-1381,[96] Genoa was able to build a maritime commercial empire that extended all the way from the Levant to the coasts of Spain. As they did this, they also fortified their control of the Italian mainland territory of Liguria and the nearby island of Corsica.[97]

The early 12th century marked the beginning of the first golden age of Genoa. In this period, its future of commercial innovation became apparent, as it started to show signs of becoming a crucial trade link between the rest of Europe and the Eastern world.[98] The city had also started to shift its form of governance - as central authority in northern Italy was beginning its collapse, the newfound vacuum of power allowed local aristocrats to assume governmental roles. As more cities in Italy were becoming republics, Genoa developed a new powerful ruling body known as a *compagna* ("those who break bread together"), and the compagna's main job was to ensure the public had specific goods for a certain period of time, whether it was to maintain a fleet of ships to make sure people had certain public goods or deal with maintaining law and order. This array of powers made the *compagna* an important tool of institutional enforcement, and the *compagna* was also important because it helped start to regularize weights and measurements, establishing legal precedents which formed a solid basis for the Genoese trading system. It also helped to usher the Republic into a new, dynamic medieval economy on strong footing. Thanks to its ability to link Western Europe to the luxurious goods of the East, Genoa found itself at the heart

---

[96] One of the most gripping conflicts of the Late Middle Ages pitted *La Superba* against *La Serenissima*, two quintessential maritime trading empires that rose to prominence roughly at the same time. See Walton, 45-54.
[97] Kirk, 9.
[98] Walton, xi.

of this flourishing economic system by the early 12th century.[99]

By the end of the 12th century, the Genoese colonial and commercial system had its principal elements firmly in place. Thanks to a comprehensive network of ships that were able to reach every part of the Mediterranean, the city developed and was in control of numerous thriving merchant colonies which had trading privileges in the East. To go along with this newfound power, the Genoese were not reluctant to use force to impose their will, which enabled them to open new markets, maintain their current routes, and establish trading outposts.[100]

Thanks to this strategy, by the end of the 13th century, the Republic of Genoa had founded colonies all around the Black Sea and the Sea of Azov, as well as in the Aegean, and on Cyprus.[101] It also was able to establish further merchant colonies on the Iberian Peninsula as well as in England and in Flanders. Contrary to what one might imagine when thinking about a colonial relationship, in the case of Genoa, the relationship between the colony and the mother city was often rather flexible, albeit not because of any largesse on the part of the Republic. Instead, it was because the reach of the empire was so expansive that stricter control was virtually impossible. Although merchants sought to maintain contact across the empire, the element that held the whole system together was the fleet of Genoese ships. At this time, there still was almost no contact via inland methods; even in surrounding Liguria, no roads linked the various Genoese coastal towns, but instead, only maritime routes.[102]

At the turn of the 14th century, Genoa's fortunes were on the upswing, but it is during this time that Genoa began to acquire its reputation for avarice and ingenuity. Liguria offered little in the way of raw materials to trade, so Genoa had to take advantage of the available silver from Sardinia and take it east to trade it. The Genoese also began to capitalize on the opportunity to trade slaves, and human beings soon became the biggest commodity being trafficked from the rural Western Mediterranean to the East. The proud, liberty-loving Genoese managed to turn the suffering of others into handsome profits for the Republic all the while.[103]

In the High Middle Ages, the Republic of Genoa was largely an urban space with a relatively modest territorial area. Its urban center was narrow, and its bustling port was surrounded by crowded neighborhoods. This environment, where people of all social classes rubbed elbows, was rife with ideas that would position Genoa at the forefront of several political and social movements. In particular, it was a setting where trade and economic expansion became a standard practice, and various social classes (aristocrats, merchants, and sailors) collaborated on

---

[99] Walton, 17.
[100] Kirk, 10.
[101] See Evgeny Khvalkov, *The Colonies of Genoa in the Black Sea Region: Evolution and Transformation.* (London: Routledge, 2017).
[102] Kirk, 10-11. One exception is in the case of Corsica, where the Genoese were able to penetrate into the interior—but it took them centuries to do so, particularly because the Genoese were often at war with Pisa over control of Corsica.
[103] Walton, 13. See also Olgiati and Zappia.

economic activities, not only in their personal interest, but also in the interest of the city.[104] In the 15th century, liberty for the citizens of Genoa meant the freedom to pursue private enterprise and the creation of wealth without any obstacle, and the commercial activities in its port and in its colonies reflected this ideology.[105]

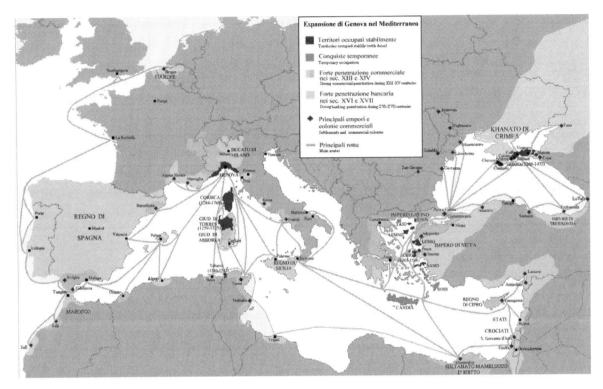

A map of Genoan spheres of influence at the end of the 14th century

In the Late Middle Ages, the businessmen of Genoa were able to construct a far reaching, intercontinental network that bore the hallmarks of their resourceful people: adaptability. Capable of efficiently transforming itself in response to any shift in the geopolitical framework, the Genoese network provided the city with the mental and financial capital that laid the groundwork for Genoa's important alliance with the Spanish.[106]

Due to the complexity of its trade networks, it is impossible to characterize the mercantile practices of the Genoese people in one single way. Historians have settled on the concept of an "emporium," which works to describe a gateway to trade whose main goal was economic success, rather than control of new territories (as would be the case in a "colonial" enterprise").[107] The three most important eastern trade destinations for Genoa were Oltremare, Alexandria, and

---

[104] Salonia, xi.
[105] Salonia, 87.
[106] Salonia, 3.
[107] Catia Brilli, *Genoese Trade and Migration in the Spanish Atlantic, 1700–1830* (Cambridge, UK: Cambridge University Press, 2016), 6. On the problems defining Genoa's status, see also Airaldi, *Genova e Liguria Nel Medioevo*.

Romania.[108] To the south, the Genoese traded with North Africa, all the way from Tunis in the west to Bougie, Ceuta, and Safi on the Atlantic. Sicily, Naples, and Sardinia were all risky ventures for Genoa in the Late Middle Ages due to their conflicts with other regional powers, including the Vatican and the Pisan Empire.[109] In their own neighborhood, Genoa also traded with Provence and Champagne, particularly in cloth, but this relationship was rocky because it depended on whether Genoa was in a state of war or peace with France.[110]

Thus, the Genoese colonies and their home port were places where people were able to encounter others and to enrich themselves. Unlike the Renaissance courts that flourished in other Italian cities at the time, the Genoese colonies and port became symbols of positive economic entanglement. They boasted a cosmopolitan environment that brought together merchants from across the world, and everything about Genoese culture in the Renaissance was pragmatic and proudly unpretentious.

It was in this context that a boy named Cristoforo Colombo was born in Genoa to a modest family.[111] The lively, atmosphere of constant dynamic exchange with the outside world, along with the unusual cargos of brightly colored fabric, rich grains and aromatic spices, understandably inspired the young boy, and in this milieu, it is not surprising that Columbus chose the life that he did. While in other parts of Europe (including Spain), a young man seeking adventure might have opted for a military career, seafaring and trade were an obvious choice in Genoa, which even had its own small colonies in the Greek islands. Columbus later claimed to have first gone to sea at the age of 10, but his first known voyages were on merchant ships to the island of Chios, a Genoese colony in the Aegean Sea which was a port of entry to the Eastern Mediterranean, which in turn was the nearest point of arrival of exotic products from Asia.

Columbus was also born around the time of the fall of Constantinople to the Ottoman Turks, whose newly powerful empire threatened trade routes to Asia. In the environment in which he grew up, there were immediate reasons, both economic and religious, to be concerned about the new balance of power. On the economic front, for several centuries, Italian merchants had been able to travel safely to the East and bring back valuable trade goods (the most famous of these was Marco Polo, whose accounts of various Asian kingdoms Columbus read). Now, having conquered Constantinople, the Muslim Turks were dangerously positioned to dominate the highly lucrative trade with the East. Meanwhile, on the religious front, the Ottomans were now not only in control of the holy city of Jerusalem but threatening the Southeastern quadrant of Christendom via their new foothold on the European continent. Both commercial and religious leaders were beginning to call for a new crusade to reestablish Christian control in the East. For some, the rising Muslim power was a sign of the coming apocalypse, anticipating the final

---

[108] Epstein, 141.
[109] Epstein, 143.
[110] Epstein, 144.
[111] On the life of Columbus see William D. Phillips and Carla Rahn Phillips, The Worlds of Christopher Columbus (Cambridge: Cambridge University Press, 1992), 85-111.

struggle between Christ and the Antichrist.

In any case, the economic goal of extending trade routes and the religious goal of expanding Christendom would remain intertwined in Columbus's later activities. A further effect of the fall of Constantinople was the arrival to Italy of thousands of Christian refugees from the former Byzantium, including Greek-speaking scholars carrying with them classical Greek manuscripts. By most accounts, their arrival was one of the major catalysts for the Italian Renaissance, and the new availability of scholarship would exercise an influence on people across Italy.

In his early expeditions, Columbus sailed as far north as the ports of Bristol, England and Galway, Ireland, and possibly even all the way to Iceland, and these trips would crucially shift his orientation from the Mediterranean to the Atlantic, a sphere of travel and trade that had been unfamiliar to him when growing up in Genoa. His realignment toward the Atlantic, and thus toward the West, was completed when he settled in Portugal around 1476, which is somewhat ironic given that Columbus started looking west as the Portuguese were fixated on looking east. His arrival in Portugal was initially accidental, according to most reports - although Genoa was at peace with Portugal, his ship, bound to England, was attacked and destroyed just beyond the Straits of Gibraltar, and Columbus was reportedly forced to come to shore clinging to an oar. The castaway was treated well by the Portuguese villagers he met on shore, and he proceeded to Lisbon, Portugal's capital, where he fell in with the city's small community of Genoese merchants and sailors.

On the one hand, Genoa in the Late Middle Ages era paints a dynamic, robust image, providing a fertile ground for some of its most promising endeavors to take root. On the other hand, however, there was also a dark side, because as the most powerful families of Genoa began to prosper in the developing empire, society also tended to become more clannish. With that, the Genoese began to earn a richly deserved reputation for being backstabbers. The city broke into multiple fiefdoms that represented the individual clans, and one example of these rivalries still visible today is the dense concentration of towers that crowd the city, each one taller than the next. The towers became sites of fighting, and competing fiefdoms would go to great lengths to destroy each other's towers. In order to stop the constant chaos, in 1196 the city had to impose a limit on the height of the towers, and authorities threatened the destruction of towers as a punishment for bad behavior.[112]

---

[112] Walton, 18.

David Bjorgen's picture of the Galata Tower built by the Genoese in Constantinople during the late 14th century

While this expensive, ostentatious rivalry between fiefdoms paints a dark picture of Genoa, the religious and charitable aspects of the people also shine through during this time. As the rich got richer, there were countless citizens left behind in poverty, and the most virtuous of the Genoese people helped create novel forms of charitable institutions in order to help raise up their fellow citizens.[113] For instance, in the late 12th century, the Genoese founded the Commenda, a hospital for pilgrims returning from the Holy Land.[114] Another measure of the charitable nature of the Genoese can be found in the records of wills left behind in the archives, which reveal an increase in such charitable donations. The women of Genoa contributed in large measure to this practice, as they financed hospitals, monasteries, Masses and churches. Other charitable donations were used to pay the ransom of captives who had been caught by marauding pirates.[115]

---

[113] Walton, 21.
[114] Walton, 21-22.
[115] Epstein, 129-30. By the late thirteenth century, however, women's rights in Genoa were on the decline which meant they were able to make fewer wills and commercial contracts. They did continue dominating charitable giving, particularly sponsoring female causes like helping widows and orphans. Epstein, 186.

By the mid-13th century, Genoa boasted a population of around 50,000 people, which made it one of the largest cities in all of Europe, behind only Paris and Venice. This period, which lasted until 1311, represented an apex in the city's history. It was a time of peace and well-being, and a time of charitable giving that reflected the strongly developed sense of communal identity. The city was able to fend off its enemies and emerge victorious in conflict after conflict, but the problems of factionalism and an overly specialized economy festered under the surface and would soon come to a head.[116] In fact, one reason for the break in the city's prosperity was a long period of civil war from 1314-1331, during which Genoa was hit by food shortages and subjected to internecine massacres.[117]

After the relative period of prosperity in the Late Middle Ages, which has received significant historical attention, the archival record of the city of Genoa becomes much less clear. No contemporary intellectuals were writing about the history of Genoa, precisely at a moment when many were focusing attention on Pisa, Florence, and Venice, cities that were experiencing their own golden ages at this time.[118] Then, in 1348, Genoa was hit by a plague that killed around 33% of Italy's population. To this day, little is known regarding how the disease hit Genoa, but modern historians estimate that the population had reached between 60,000 and 65,000 people on the eve of the plague. By 1350, imports and food consumption had declined between 30-50%, which indicated the population had been reduced dramatically.[119]

While it is safe to say that the plague represented a traumatic moment for all of Europe, there was one benefit for the city of Genoa in that it allowed for a brief truce with the Republic of Venice, the other great maritime superpower of the period.[120] Nonetheless, that benefit was to be short lived, as not even mass death could stop the rivalry between the two. By 1370, Genoa was back at work, figuring out how to defeat the Venetians definitively.

The two cities had been at odds for several centuries by this point. In an effort to counter the Venetians' rising fortunes, Byzantine leaders established new trading agreements with Genoa and Pisa in 1169 and 1170. In 1171, Byzantine authorities demanded the confiscation of all goods and commodities in an effort to target every last one of the Venetian merchants in the empire. This put the Italian powers at odds, and by the start of the 14th century, the Venetian Arsenal was pumping out dozens of galleys as Venice braced for war.

The final major war between the two began in Cyprus, as groups of Venetians and Genoese began skirmishes that soon ballooned into a full-fledged war. At this point, Genoa controlled both the spice and grain trade, bringing in goods from distant regions, including India, so Venice

---

[116] Epstein, 138-139.
[117] Walton, 93.
[118] Epstein, 188.
[119] Epstein, 214.
[120] Jeffrey Miner and Stefan Stantchev. "The Genoese Economy," In *A Companion to Medieval Genoa*, edited by Carrie E. Benes. Leiden and Boston: BRILL Press, 2018), 397.

allied with Pisa against Genoa. Genoa looked to the king of Hungary and the city of Padua for assistance, but the Venetians were determined to hold out. In 1380, the Genoese collapsed, allowing Venice to declare victory thanks to their superior unity. That said, the victory was not complete, as Genoa had managed to enter all the way into Venice's Lagoon, and the final balance of power at the end of the war was not dramatically altered.[121] Nonetheless, the War of Chioggia led to the signing in 1381 of the Peace of Turin, an agreement that marked the decline of the Genoese influence on the Mediterranean. Having triumphed over its rival, Venice was granted supreme dominion over its waters.

The reason the hostilities between the two empires ceased afterwards had less to do with any interests in keeping the peace, and more to do with the fact that both were in their decline. In fact, neither would be able to consider itself a superpower after the conflict, and the damage that each inflicted on the other was compounded by the fact that their war had distracted them from the rise of the Ottoman Empire.[122]

The End of the Middle Ages

Historians depict the end of the Middle Ages as a transitional period for Venice, sandwiched between the Byzantine imperial phase and the more Roman-inspired imperial age of Venice that followed.[123] In the 14th century, Venetian enterprises continued to expand, and the growth and consolidation of urban Venice continued unabated throughout the century.[124] Inspired by fierce competition with their Genoese rivals, Venetian explorers began searching out new markets by sea as well as by land."[125] Other elements of Venetian culture were stabilized during this time. For instance, the Venetians formalized the celebration of their Carnevale event, when the Senate of the Republic declared it would be observed officially on the last day of Lent.

The trade Venice conducted over land was bolstered in part by the exploits of one of its most famous native sons. Relatively early in the city's history, Venetian traders and other European traders began to maintain trade relationships with traders on the Silk Road, an overland trade route that linked China and the Mediterranean. The Silk Road encompassed both the Far East and Near East, including Beijing and Baghdad, and traders moved goods from east to west and west to east. Prior to the Mongol conquests, the route was relatively dangerous and frequently plagued by thieves, high tolls and other challenges. While the Venetians did not travel the Silk Road, they did have contacts in North Africa and elsewhere with caravan traders.

---

[121] Musarra, 142-143.
[122] Walton, 59-60. Musarra calls the Ottomans the "true" victors of the war. Musarra, 143.
[123] Chambers, 20.
[124] Crouzet-Pavan, *Venice Triumphant*, 12.
[125] Strathern, 6.

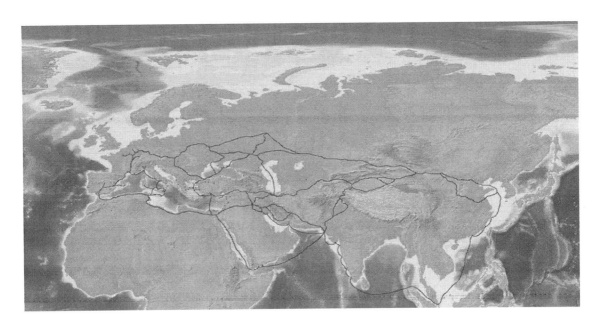

A map of overland trade routes used in the 9th century by the Radhanites

During the course of the 13th century, the Mongols conquered much of the eastern world under Genghis Khan, who united a huge portion of the eastern world by forcefully subduing and taking large regions. In areas that simply surrendered, violence was limited and local governors were allowed to retain their roles. At its height, the Mongolian Empire controlled more than 9 million square miles and 100 million people, and upon Genghis Khan's death, his empire was split between his grandsons. While the Mongolians did not maintain the unity of their empire, they continued to provide a sort of Pax Mongolica, even while separated into four distinct khanates. During his reign, Kublai Khan fought others in his family dynasty to retain his power, having been elected Great Khan alongside his brother. Over time, Kublai Khan consolidated and expanded his empire.

Kublai Khan

As Great Khan, Kublai Khan ruled the Mongolian Empire from his capital in modern-day Beijing, with a court that included Mongolians, Arabs, and Persians from throughout his empire. While Genghis Khan may have been a warrior, Kublai Khan was a man of culture, intellect and curiosity, and his court was a luxurious one rich in art, music, and goods.

Under the rule of the Mongolian Empire, trade along the Silk Road was both easier and more efficient than ever before. Toll gates were removed and traders could move freely from place to place. It was said that even women could travel safely with goods without fear of harm. Most importantly, the Mongolian emperors welcomed foreigners and traders in their empire and their courts.

One of Kublai Khan's most famous contemporaries was none other than a Venetian traveler named Marco Polo. The Polo family first appears in Venetian records in the late 10th century, and they were apparently already wealthy mine owners during this time, as well as regular travelers between Venice and Dalmatia on the eastern coast of the Adriatic (in modern day Croatia). Members of the Polo family were among the nobility and commanding ships for the Republic by the 12th century. Thus, by the time the two Polo brothers (Marco's father and uncle) set off on their journey, they had the financial and social standing required to make such a trip.

Niccolò and Maffeo Polo were Venetian merchants and noblemen who eventually established successful trading facilities in the Crimean port of Soldaia (modern-day Suldak), Constantinople and a western trading post in the Mongol empire. During the 1250s, the pair left Venice for

Constantinople, leaving behind their families. When they left, Niccolò's wife was either pregnant or had just given birth to an infant son.

   Though the Byzantine Empire still existed in the 13th century, it was a shell of its former self, and Constantinople had been taken by the Venetians in 1204, maintaining a substantial Venetian presence thereafter. Niccolò and Maffeo likely felt at home in the city when they arrived, and the two remained in Constantinople until 1259 or 1260. At that time, political tensions in the region made a move essential because the Ottoman Turks were attempting to take Constantinople. As it turned out, the Venetian quarter in Constantinople was destroyed soon after the Polos departed. While they planned to return to Venice, pirates in the Black Sea blocked their path, so they moved on, establishing the family business in Soldaia. Soldaia, located in Crimea, was under the control of the Mongol state at the time and thus part of the Mongol Golden Horde.

15th century manuscript depicting the Polo brothers leaving Constantinople and heading east

While the pope had denounced the violent actions of his grandfather, Kublai Khan's empire was remarkably peaceful and, even by Western standards, quite civilized. Kublai Khan received the Polo brothers with great curiosity, provided them with lavish quarters, and asked many questions about life in the West, particularly about Christianity and the Catholic Church. While the Polo brothers likely believed they were the first Europeans in the khan's court, there had been other traders, merchants and knights in the past. Kublai Khan's court welcomed foreigners, but retained a strong Mongol identity even in China.

Niccolò and Maffeo returned to Venice in 1269 or 1270; and upon coming home they learned the papal elections were quite delayed. Thus, they were not able to deliver the message from Kublai Khan until after the next papal election in 1271, and they eventually opted to continue on their mission regardless of the situation with the papacy. Marco Polo is believed to have been about 15 years old when his father returned, and he was apparently considered old enough to join his father and uncle on their second journey east to the court of the Khan two years after their return. While Niccolò and Maffeo had made a rather haphazard and slow trip east the first time, this time they hadt he advantage of traveling with the paiza. Having made the acquaintance of the new pope, Pope Gregory X, the three traveled first to part of modern-day Lebanon to speak to the papal legate in the Kingdom of Acre. They had made the acquaintance of Teobaldo Visconti on their earlier journey. From there, they were allowed to travel to Jerusalem in search of the oil of the Holy Sepulchre requested by Kublai Khan.

Marco, Niccolò and Maffeo returned to Venice permanently changed by their journey to the Khan's lands. Having been gone for over two decades, they could barely speak their native language after years without practice. They wore Mongol-style clothing, including brightly colored caftans, layered over loose-fitting trousers. They may even have worn their hair in the Mongol style, with parts of the head shaved and long braids. They were not recognized when they arrived home, and their family in Venice had no way of knowing if they were alive or dead and likely assumed them dead after so many years.

Niccolò and Maffeo's brother had made provisions for them in his will before his death, and when they returned they were immediately made the executors of his estate. This measure provided the returning members of the family with the legal standing that they needed in the city. Maffeo's wife was alive, as was Niccolò's second son, Maffeo Polo. Still facing doubt, the three threw a grand banquet. During the course of the banquet, according to legend, they tore apart multiple sets of rich clothing before finally appearing in their Mongol caftans. They cut into the caftans, revealing rich stores of gems and gold sewn into the fabric. Only after this display were they welcomed back into Venetian society.

However, Marco brought knowledge of a number of significant technological advances back to Italy with him, including paper money, coal and eyeglasses. The eyeglass lenses also provided the innovation necessary for the telescope, and the introduction of gunpowder revolutionized warfare. He kept the paiza, given by Kublai Khan, for the rest of his life and was served by a Mongol servant named Peter in his home in Venice.

While Venice had been a thriving republic when Marco left 24 years earlier, he returned to a less successful city. Under interdict by the Pope for some time, the city could not even celebrate religious festivals, and wars and famine also threatened the city. The people of Venice blamed members of the ruling families, particularly the Dandolo family, for their difficulties. Making matters worse, the Christian kingdom of Acre, where the Polos had began their journey, had fallen to the sultan of Egypt, so a lack of Christian trading outposts in the Middle East reduced

Venetian access to trade in the region. In response, the Venetians increased trade throughout western Europe.

Sometime after Marco's return to the city, tensions between Venice and longtime trading rival, Genoa escalated. Genoa controlled both the spice and grain trade, bringing in goods from distant regions, including India. Venice allied with Pisa against Genoa and initiated a draft. All men between 17-60 could be drafted, and Marco volunteered to serve. Clearly not a prime age for fighting by now, Marco may simply have found Venice boring after a life of travel and adventure.

During the naval battle with the city of Genoa, Marco Polo was captured and taken prisoner, but like other wealthy prisoners, he was quite well-treated and his prison was a luxurious one. His family in Venice worried about his well-being, and Niccolò and Maffeo attempted to ransom him to secure his freedom. With concern about Marco's well-being and the family's future, Niccolò remarried. While Marco was in prison, the family bought a new palazzo in a comfortable Venetian neighborhood. The gems and goods brought from the east likely financed this purchase.

In prison, Marco met a writer of adventure stories and romances named Rustichello of Pisa who had likely been captured by the Genoese in 1284 and had been imprisoned for a number of years. While Marco spoke a number of languages, none, including his native Venetian, were appropriate for a literary venture, but Rustichello was fluent in French, a popular literary language of the time.

While in prison, Marco, with Rustichello's assistance, began work on the book about his travels. This autobiography included many stories of Marco's travels throughout the Mongol kingdom, as well as those of his father and uncle. He also included second-hand accounts of a number of regions and some stories which were, without a doubt, purely fictional. Marco dictated his autobiography to Rustichello, and the two should be considered co-writers, but as the book progresses it moves further from conventions of travel and adventure stories. This suggests that Marco may have taken a greater hand in its writing, and Marco may have relied upon some of his own travel notes, as well as his memory, when dictating his adventures to Rustichello.

While Rustichello could write French, he did so poorly. Verb tenses varied, and he moved from first to third person narration frequently. The poor grammar and language of the text subsequently caused substantial difficulties for translators. The original manuscript produced by Rustichello in prison does not survive, and early surviving copies vary widely, with alterations to the text in many instances. Modern scholars divide these manuscripts into two groups, A and B. Manuscripts in the B group are believed to be truer to the original and less altered by translators. Marco may have added to the manuscript later in life, continuing to alter the text until the time of his death.

119 early manuscripts of the Travels of Marco Polo survive, but only a few circulated in Venice. Nobles, scholars, and monks were the first readers of the text, but many who could not read may have also learned of Marco's travels orally. The Travels may have been translated into Tuscan within just years of its writing. A Dominican monk, Francesco Pipino, translated the text into Latin between 1310 and 1314. His translation edited the text for a religious audience, removing sexual references and providing the Travels of Marco Polo with a distinctly Christian perspective. It later appeared in German, English, Catalan, Aragonese, Venetian, Latin and even Gaelic. Circulation increased after the invention of the movable printing press. The first printed text appeared in 1477 in Germany, followed by another German edition four years later. Pipino's Latin translation provided the basis for a French translation in the 16th century.

Even as Marco Polo's account began the process of making its way across Europe, the Venetians widely considered him a fiction writer at best by the end of his life, and that perception continued into the 14th century. Even translators believed the stories to be fictional, because other adventure and travel stories, like that of John Mandeville, were pure fiction. Mandeville simply combined stories, often relying upon ancient sources, and he had not traveled on his own. Mandeville's account of his imagined travels was more popular than Marco Polo's for many years, and the two were frequently grouped together.

The Travels of Marco Polo includes Marco's factual observations, noting plants, animals and people that he saw with his own eyes. In the text, he insists that he was present at certain times and places. While descriptions of his own experiences can mostly be considered truthful, he also includes other information that he certainly believed to be true, including second-hand information, local mythology and his own opinions. The role he played in the Mongol court enabled him to provide observations about the character and personality of the ruler, Kublai Khan. To understand why so many thought Marco Polo had written fiction, it's necessary to keep in mind that he was not only trying to create a factual account but an imaginative and exciting text describing his travels and journeys.

In 1492, Columbus carried a copy of the Travels of Marco Polo on his journeys to the New World. He hoped to find Marco Polo's China and its rich trade goods, including spices that Marco mentioned in his accounts of India. This edition exists today and is heavily annotated in his own hand. A later Venetian explorer, Antonio Pigafetta, circumnavigated the globe and wrote his own account of his voyage, inspired by Polo's writing.

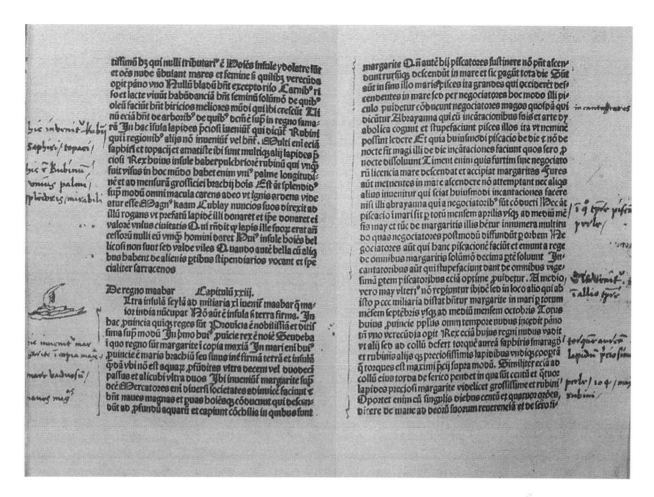

Columbus' notes in Latin on the margins of his copy of *The Travels of Marco Polo*

By the 17th century, Marco Polo was much more well-regarded and often referred to as the one "who discovered new countries". He appeared in an ecclesiastical history of Venice late in the 17th century, and during the early 19th century, Marco Polo's accounts were recognized as fundamentally factual. Scholars compared the *Travels of Marco Polo* to annals of the Mongol and Chinese courts and found clear similarities in the depiction of court rituals, merchant practices, and religion. Large annotated editions of the *Travels* appeared and became popular in the 19th century.

By the time of his death, Polo's Venice was a bustling port city, and much of its prosperity was due to the diversity of its inhabitants, including mainland farmers wearing their traditional peasant dress, Arab merchants wearing turbans and djellabas; Slavs and Albanians wearing traditional tribal baggy trousers; and Jews wearing their long dark gaberdine cloaks. For all the diversity, the city retained its core identity as a Christian place of rather strict Christian morality. One unusual exception to this, however, were the surprising number of courtesans and prostitutes in Venice, where prostitution was actually encouraged, insofar as authorities thought it would discourage homosexuality. The Republic strictly regulated prostitutes' activities, making the practice one of economic benefit that brought in quite a bit of money to the Republic's exchequer.[126] In addition to the common prostitute, there was an unusual figure known as the "honest" courtesan, who was ambiguously also a society lady paid for her attention. Courtesans enjoyed great reputations and openly attended social gatherings without any threat of moral censure. Venetian courtesans were highly appreciated for their witty and clever banter, as well as their beauty, but they also helped contribute to the spread of syphilis in Venice around this time. Courtesans were also popular because marriage was relatively rare in Venice at the time. Since women were expected to bring a hefty dowry to their husband, many were unmarried and ended up becoming nuns.[127]

In the mid-14th century, Venice and the rest of Europe would be rocked by something completely beyond their control or understanding. Survival depended, for the most part, on working with nature to grow enough food to eat during the summer and save for the winter to survive. When nature cooperated, there might be more to eat or even a little bit to sell for something else, but when it did not cooperate, people died in large numbers. Therefore, there was a lot of interest in ensuring the type of good crop that would lead to survival, even if people weren't sure exactly how or whether there was actually a way to do so. Europe was a highly Christian continent at the time, with the Catholic Church one of its most powerful forces, so men like Mussis attributed the spread of the plague to the Earth working in concert with God against mankind: "And the earth replied, 'I, established by your power, shall open and swallow up the countless criminals as soon as you give the word. When the enraged judge gives the signal, with violent thunder from heaven, and leads the elements, the planets, the stars and the orders of angels against the human race in an unspeakable judgment, enlisting all forms of life to wipe out the sinners at one savage stroke, I shall refuse the usual harvest, I shall not yield grain, win or oil.'"

One of the ways in which people tried to ensure that the forces of nature would be on their side was by placating a God that they often viewed as vengeful and hard to understand. In the 14th century, people were intimately familiar with the kind and gentle teachings of Jesus Christ found in the New Testament, but they were also aware of the warnings of God's wrath spelled out in the Old Testament. As a result, when something went wrong, the assumption was that God was angry and people were getting their just desserts. Likewise, when there was a bountiful crop, people assumed it was because God was pleased and chose to bless the people. In both cases, religion in Europe during the Middle Ages made many people superstitious, as evidenced by what Mussis wrote: "We know that whatever we suffer is the just reward of our sins. Now, therefore, when the Lord is enraged, embrace acts of penance, so that you do not stray from the right path and perish. Let the proud be humbled. Let misers, who withheld alms from the poor.

---

[126] Strathern, 218.
[127] Strathern, 219. For more on women in the Republic of Venice, see Federica Ambrosini, "Toward a Social History of Women in Venice. From the Renaissance to the Enlightenment." In *Venice Reconsidered. The History and Civilization of an Italian City-State, 1297-1797,* edited by John Martin and Dennis Romano. Baltimore, MD and London: The Johns Hopkins University Press, 2000, 420-453.

Blush for shame. Let the envious become zealous in almsgiving. Let lechers put aside their filthy habits and distinguish themselves in honest living. Let the raging and wrathful restrain themselves from violence. … Let all of you hurry to set your feet on the way of salvation."

The Black Death certainly seemed to be some form of retribution because it appeared to have arrived from the East, a place the European Catholics considered pagan. Today it's apparent that the disease was not the result of an evil plot put together by the enemies of Christianity but almost certainly carried by rats infested with fleas. Still, many sailors returning to Europe from voyages to either Asia or the Middle East likely did bring the sickness with them, a fact that Mussis pointed out: "Thus almost everyone who had been in the East, or in the regions to the south and north, fell victim to sudden death after contracting this pestilential disease, as if struck by lethal arrow which raised a tumor on their bodies. The scale of the mortality and the form which it too persuaded those who lived, weeping and lamenting, through the bitter events of 1346 to 1348—the Chinese, Indians, Persians, Medes, Kurds, Armenians, Cilicians, Georgians, Mesopotamians, Nubians, Ethiopians, Turks, Egyptians, Arabs, Saracens and Greeks (for almost all the East had been affected)—that the last judgment had come."

For many years, scientists have believed that the Black Death was a form of the bubonic plague, a deadly illness carried and spread by fleas found on rodents. The belief was that rats covered with the fleas traveled west on boats to Europe, where they reproduced and spread their infected parasites to humans, who subsequently contracted the plague and died. However, given the different strains and symptoms found across Europe, it has been alternatively suggested that the Black Death that attacked Europe during the 1340s and 1350s might also have been caused by an airborne pathogen of some sort, and this was certainly the belief that those afraid of the disease embraced.

A depiction of the plague in Florence as described by *The Decameron*

A medieval depiction of Boccaccio and other Florentines fleeing the plague

Though it most likely began in Asia, the plague was first observed in Europe in the southern tip of France and much of Greece in 1347, and from there, it spread north into the rest of France and Italy in 1348. By 1349, it had reached England and Germany, and it arrived in Russia in late 1349, yet by the time it reached Denmark in 1350, the disease had mostly disappeared in the first countries it had affected.

The first recorded death from the plague in Venice occurred on January 25, 1348, and by the summer of that year, an estimated 600 people were dying each day.[128] Although it is impossible to know how many died, scholars estimate that it would have probably been around a third of the total population, and unfortunately, the diversity of Venice and its role as a crossroads ended up causing it to suffer more profoundly than other cities that had a less active exchange of peoples.

Although these outbreaks of the Black Death continued at least once a decade, the Venetians were quick to rebound, and their trading levels were soon restored to the levels from before the plague.[129] The Black Death also slowed the city's physical expansion, which had continued at a very speedy rate up to the early 1340s, peaking in 1343. The land reclamation projects only resumed at their former intensity in 1385.

Venice was able to fill the gap of human labor caused by the widespread decimation of the population thanks to its connections to the slave trade. Venice was positioned to provide new, healthy bodies to the desperate cities, and although slavery had been banned by church for centuries, after the plague those prohibitions were widely ignored because of the desperation and chaos. Venice imported Slavic, Caucasian, Armenian and Georgian slaves, as well as Nubians, earning the Venetian traders as much as 1000% profits.[130] With this abundant source of income and healthy manpower, Venetian production was able to boom, and in the wake of the plague, the city invented a kind of assembly line production system, about 600 years before Henry Ford made it famous with the Model T cars.[131]

Another benefit of the plague was that it brought about a truce with the rival Genoese empire. However, the truce lasted barely two years before they were back to fighting on the Dalmatian front.[132] The conflict with Genoa only came to a definitive end with the war of Chioggia (1378-1381). This led to the Peace of Turin, signed in 1381, a treatise that marked the decline of the Genoese influence on the Mediterranean. Having triumphed over its rival, Venice was granted supreme dominion over its waters. Then, in the wake of the War of Chioggia, Venice decided to turn its efforts to conquering more of mainland Italy, annexing Carrara, Vicenza and Padua in 1405.[133] By 1423, the Italian territory governed by Venice actually stretched all the way from the hills behind Verona to the Julian Alps.[134]

With these major conquests began the imperial period of Venice. From 1380 onward, Venice increased its direct control over the Italian *terraferma* at an even faster rate than it increased its overseas empire.[135] Its influence on the peninsula ranked it alongside the major cities of Naples,

---

[128] Strathern, 24.
[129] Strathern, 26.
[130] Strathern, 26.
[131] Strathern, 26.
[132] Strathern, 30; Dalmatia is one of the four historical regions of Croatia, on the eastern shore of the Adriatic sea.
[133] Strathern, 73; Carrara is a coastal city in Tuscany, famous for its marble quarries. Padua is a city nearby to Venice, famous for its university.
[134] Chambers, 58.

Rome, Florence and Milan, and its population had finally managed to recover from the plague, with over 100,000 people calling Venice home.[136] This made Venice a larger city than either London or Paris at that time.

Genoa's Golden Age

With the benefit of hindsight, there are clear signs that Genoa had reached a downturn after the War of Chioggia with Venice in the late 14th century, but historians point to a second upswing, "the century of the Genoese," that came in the 16th century. In the 1550s, Genoa began to acquire a position of superiority in European finance and an influential status in European affairs in general.

In 1407, Genoa established one of the first banks in the history of the world. The Casa di San Giorgio, a bank formed by a group of creditors who pledged to manage the Republic's debts, predated the illustrious Bank of England by three centuries.[137] This bank allowed Genoese investors who came from diverse economic and social backgrounds to gain healthy returns on their capital and make sure that the money was tied up so that the commune could not pressure them to overspend on risky military adventures that might threaten their commercial interests.[138] This leadership in banking paid the city dividends during the "century of the Genoese."[139] In fact, thanks to the existence of the Casa di San Giorgio, the financial practices in Genoa had become so sophisticated and so widespread among the elite that by 1500, the key conditions were in place for Genoa to become the most important lender to the Spanish Empire.[140] Later, under the guidance of visionary Andrea Doria (discussed further below), the quantity of loans that Genoese financiers made to Holy Roman Emperor Charles V surpassed those made by German bankers, eventually representing more than 50% of all loans made to the emperor.[141] Machiavelli wrote of the bank, "This establishment presents an instance of what in all the republics, either described or imagined by philosophers, has never been thought of; exhibiting within the same community, and among the same citizens, liberty and tyranny, integrity and corruption, justice and injustice; for this establishment preserves in the city many ancient and venerable customs; and should it happen (as in time it easily may) that the San Giorgio should

---

[135] Chambers, 54.
[136] At its largest, Venice's population reached 170,000 people and had more than two million in its territorial empire. Martin and Romano, "Reconsidering Venice, " 1.
[137] Walton, 93. Such was the wonder of the bank that Machiavelli himself took notice and referred to it with admiration in his history of Florence. Bent, 220.
[138] Salonia, xvi.
[139] Kirk, 29. See also Henri Lapeyre, "La participation des genois aux 'asientos' de Charles Quint et de Philippe II." In R. Belvederi, ed., *Rapporti Genova-Mediterraneo-Atlantico, Atti del Congresso Internazionale di studi storici* (Genoa: University of Genoa, 1983), 152-3. Kirk suggests that the end of Genoese supremacy, between 1607 to the late 1640s, can be marked by when the Spanish began to surpass them in their loans.
[140] Miner and Stantchev, 417.
[141] Kirk, 29. See also Henri Lapeyre, "La participation des genois aux 'asientos' de Charles Quint et de Philippe II." In R. Belvederi, ed., *Rapporti Genova-Mediterraneo-Atlantico, Atti del Congresso Internazionale di studi storici* (Genoa: University of Genoa, 1983), 152-3. Kirk suggests that the end of Genoese supremacy, between 1607 to the late 1640s, can be marked by when the Spanish began to surpass them in their loans.

have possession of the whole city, the republic will become more distinguished than that of Venice." Joseph Addison echoed that sentiment, writing around 1701, "I know nothing more remarkable in the government of Genoa, than the bank of St. George, made up of such branches of the revenues, as have been set apart and appropriated to the discharging of several sums, that have been borrowed from private persons, during the exigencies of the commonwealth. Whatever inconveniences the state has labored under, they have never entertained a thought of violating the public credit, or of alienating any part of these revenues to other uses, than to what they have been thus assigned. The administration of this bank is for life, and partly in the hands of the chief citizens, which gives them a great authority in the state, and a powerful influence over the common people. This bank is generally thought the greatest load on the Genoese, and the managers of it have been represented as a second kind of senate, that break the uniformity of government, and destroy in some measure the fundamental constitution of the state. It is, however, very certain, that the people reap no small advantages from it, as it distributes the power among more particular members of the republic, and gives the commons a figure: So that it is no small check upon the aristocracy, and may be one reason why the Genoese senate carries it with greater moderation towards their subjects than the Venetian."

A modern picture of the building

Charles V

The Genoese no doubt earned a great deal of money from these international loans, and they became a godsend when their naval power in the Mediterranean started to decline.[142] However, Genoa's true financial prowess was due to its status as a great port for commercial exchange[143] since its strategic position in the Mediterranean Sea meant that it was able to dominate trade between Italy and Spain.[144] Considered to be the best port between Barcelona and La Spezia, during the early 16th century, Genoese ships were able to carry between 12,000 and 15,000 tons, and the capacity reached upwards of 29,000 tons by the 1550s, effectively doubling the capacity in 50 years. By the end of the century, it was back down to below the levels of the early 1500s.[145]

---

[142] Walton, 95.

[143] Kirk, 32. See also Giacomo Casarino, *Genova, solo mercanti?: artigiani, corporazioni e manifattura tra Quattro e Cinquecento* (Rome: Aracne editrice, 2018).

[144] Giulia Bonazza, *Abolitionism and the Persistence of Slavery in Italian States, 1750-1850* (Cham, Switzerland: Palgrave Macmillan, n.d.), 140.

[145] Kirk, 33. This arc roughly matches the arc of the size of the fleet of the Republic of Venice, which was at about 15,000 at the start of the century, rose to 30,000 by mid century, and was reduced to 10,000 tons in 1605. Kirk, 35.

Genoa's status as the best port in the northern Mediterranean conferred great advantages upon the city, but it also brought the constant threat of raids from privateers.[146] In fact, the most recurrent theme found in archival documents is the urgent need to build up defenses and armaments.[147] In 1559, Genoa decided to formalize its self-protection by establishing a Magistrate Delle Galee (Office for the Galleys), whose job it was to construct an entire fleet devoted to the defense of the city.[148]

In conjunction with these efforts, one of the reasons for the "Genoese century" was the leadership of Andrea Doria (1466-1560).[149] Born into a minor branch of one of Genoa's great families, Doria was orphaned as a child and thus was sent to Rome to become a soldier in the papal guard. He spent years in central Italy as a mercenary and even made a pilgrimage to the Holy Land in 1495 before returning home, where he worked in Corsica for the Casa di San Giorgio.[150] Although it is not clear how, he managed to develop extraordinary naval skills and received a commission in the Genoese navy. Eventually, he fought against the Turks, earning recognition for his contributions to a 1516 raid against North Africa.[151]

---

[146] Bonazza, 140.
[147] Edoardo Grendi, *La Repubblica Aristocratica Dei Genovesi: Politica, Carita e Commercio Fra Cinque e Seicento* (Genoa: Il mulino, 1985), 309.
[148] Bonazza, 140.
[149] Walton, 79.
[150] Grendi, *La Repubblica Aristocratica Dei Genovesi,* 142-44.
[151] Epstein, 314.

A portrait of Doria

Aside from these military accomplishments, Doria is remembered today for his understanding of the changing world and his ability to adapt to it, earning him the anachronistic title of the "Steve Jobs" of the Mediterranean (perhaps Steve Jobs deserves to be called the Andrea Doria of Silicon Valley).[152] His main business was warfare, and his early training as a mercenary was reflected throughout his career as he wove business interests into everything he did.[153] He was savvy enough to realize that shifting trade routes in the early 16th century were altering Genoa's traditional field of operations - the Portuguese and Spanish started exploring the Atlantic, and he managed to help Genoa reposition itself in order to best take advantage of the change.[154] In 1527,

---

[152] Walton, 81.
[153] Walton, 82.

as Genoa was racked with feuds and recovering from another plague, he marched into Genoa with his army and purged the government of its warring factions. With the support of the Habsburgs in Spain, Doria took control of the city and immediately offered its new allies a line of credit they sorely needed thanks the high costs and irregular cashflow generated by the Spanish explorations of the New World.[155]

Doria lived to an extremely old age for the time (94), and he managed to command fleets against Barbary pirates into his 80s.[156] During his reign, the city of Genoa was a happy place with elaborate parties and lavish festivals as the norm, but unfortunately, as long and as successful as his life was, it only served to staunch the wound that was already bleeding in the empire. For 10 years after his death, the city enjoyed peace while concentrating their fighting on the island of Corsica, but soon internal disagreements within the city boiled up as the two factions of nobles who had been forced to accept Doria's reforms went back to war with each other. One faction sought refuge amongst the Spanish, where Doria's grandnephew, Gian Andrea Doria, was living. With the blessing of the Spanish, they returned to Genoa to seize power and established a new series of reforms, modernizing his great uncle's regime and successfully quieting discontent and restoring order.[157]

When Doria's grandnephew led a small Genoese naval contingent against the Turks at Lepanto in 1571, Genoa was on the winning side, but the bloom was already off the rose.[158] Coupled with this slow military decline, the helpfulness of being linked to Spain only lasted so long, and as soon as Spain faced its own financial trouble in the mid-1570s,[159] Genoa saw its own fortunes precipitously decline.[160] The financial hit was exacerbated by Spain's inability to keep up its patrol of the Mediterranean against pirates, which led to an upswing in raids against Liguria in the late 16th century that further hastened the end of the Genoese century and foreshadowed the end to come.[161]

The Decline of Venice

Taking care of the Genoese threat served to boost the Venetian self-image, but as soon as that threat was neutralized, they faced an even fiercer foe in the Ottoman Turks. The Ottomans were making inroads against the Byzantine Empire after conquering Thessalonica in 1430 and then Constantinople in 1453.[162] The fall of Constantinople actually served to emphasize the split between East and West, bringing to an end an extraordinary period of cultural and economic

---

[154] Walton, 92.
[155] Walton, 95.
[156] Kirk, 319. See also Bent, 300-301.
[157] Bent, 306-307.
[158] Kirk, 319. See also Walton, xiv.
[159] King Philip II suspended payment on Spanish crown debts in 1607, Kirk, 84.
[160] Walton, 95.
[161] Walton, 95-6.
[162] McGregor, 2.

exchange.[163] Moreover, this Ottoman victory meant that the Venetians lost their last barrier against a potential Islamic invasion.[164]

The collapse of the Byzantine Empire put the Venetians on the defensive and forced them to have to consolidate the defense of their Eastern territories, their Mediterranean colonies, and their lucrative trade routes. Nonetheless, despite their efforts, they still lost important lands during the late 15th century, a sign that Venice may have gotten too big for its proverbial britches. Furthermore, as the city decided to make more incursions within the Italian peninsula, the Venetians provoked the fear and ire of the ruler of Florence, Cosimo de Medici, who directed Florentine policy in a whole new direction. While the two republics had an alliance since 1425 that was meant to protect Italy's liberty against foreign invaders, Cosimo decided to break it off, which meant Florence and Venice went to war just as Constantinople was falling in the early 1450s.[165]

In 1463, with the Ottomans now the unquestionable authority in the East, the Turkish-Venetian War began, inaugurating nearly two decades of bloodshed. Venice suffered a massive blow at the beginning of the 1470s with its defeat at the Battle of Negroponte, and after being shaken by the number of warships and troops the Turkish army had unleashed upon them, Venetian authorities decided to take action at once. In 1473, the Arsenale Nuovissimo, or "Very New Arsenal," was established. To begin with, the new extension was filled with roofed berths, a shipping term for "docking site," and subsidiary structures that supported the existing weaponry and vessel manufacturing plants, including more foundries, armories, and powdering mills (where gunpowder was produced). The Nuovissimo was by far the most elaborate of all the arsenal's extensions. The new shipyard, which was about 25 hectares in size, could now handle the manufacturing of vessels that weighed over 300 tons and ran up to 165 feet from nose to tail. As usual, a row of looming defensive walls boxed in the Nuovissimo.

In January 1479, Venice signed the Treaty of Constantinople, a peace treaty with the Ottoman Empire, whose naval power was undisputable.[166] This treaty cost Venice economically, as the Venetians now had to pay the Sultan an annual fee in order to be able to trade on the Black Sea. It also cost them in terms of territory, as they also had to give up territories on the Dalmatian coast and in the Greek Isles.

At this point, Venice turned its military attention back to the Italian peninsula, initiating fruitless wars with Ferrara and the surrounding areas. Feeling this threat, the rest of the Italian states decided to band together to oppose Venetian territorial expansion, and in 1509, they formed the League of Cambrai, made up of Spain, France, Germany, the Papal States, Hungary, the Savoy and Ferrara. A French expeditionary force led an army that decisively defeated the

---

[163] Strathern, 115.
[164] McGregor, 2.
[165] Chambers, 59.
[166] Angione.

Venetians at the Battle of Agnadello on May 14 of that year, and the foreign invasions of Italy that began in 1494 dramatically set the stage for the last acts of Venetian empire-building.[167] As a result of the loss, the Venetian army was disbanded and high-profile Venetians were taken by the French as prisoners. In the words of the notorious statesman and writer Niccolo Machiavelli, "In one battle they lost what in eight hundred years they had won with so much effort."[168]

Venice was able to gradually regain the bulk of its lost territories, but in just four short years, they faced devastation once again, including losing all their Italian holdings and even having the nearby city of Mestre burned to the ground. Despite this unquestionably serious loss, the city of Venice itself remained unscathed, and accounts even claim that there was not a single incident of looting or raping during the three years of fighting that followed. In the ensuing three years, Venice successfully managed to regain its mainland territories and defend its liberty, but the lengthy conflict took a toll on the inhabitants, setting off a series of internal conflicts within the ruling elite.[169] It also opened a debate about the nature of the ideal Venetian citizen and what should be done by every individual citizen in order to protect the liberty of a republic under siege.[170]

Soon after this devastating series of defeats at home and abroad, Venice's maritime supremacy began to be seriously challenged within Europe. The Portuguese were on the rise, as demonstrated by their successful circumnavigation of the African continent, a feat that further challenged the city's old trade monopoly with the East. New trade routes opened up that quickly stripped away their monopoly, but even as they faced stiff competition on the seas, the Venetians attempted to take more territory on the Italian peninsula. Ultimately, this merely resulted in Venice being dragged into the constant bloodshed that wracked Renaissance Italy.[171]

By the 1500s, the arsenal was said to have been turning out 6 galleys a month, and when they began to accept more orders for vessels from foreign clients, this number swiftly swelled. In 1535, yet another small extension was tacked on to the northwestern end of the Nuovissimo, which became home to more powdering mills and gunpowder reservoirs. By the mid-16th century, the Arsenale family was at its height, with over 16,000 employees working there. At this point, they were grinding out 1 ship a day. To put this in perspective, building a vessel of a similar size would have taken a competitor months to complete.

Yet another legend would spawn with the new addition to the arsenal. As the story goes, when the French king Henry III visited, Alvise Mocenigo, then the reigning doge, attempted to showboat. To showcase the dazzling faculties of his illustrious shipping and armory network,

---

[167] Chambers, 61.
[168] Edward Muir, "Was There Republicanism in The Renaissance Republics? Venice after Agnadello," In *Venice Reconsidered. The History and Civilization of an Italian City-State, 1297-1797,* edited by John Martin and Dennis Romano. Baltimore, MD and London: The Johns Hopkins University Press, 2000, 138.
[169] Muir, 139.
[170] Muir, 139.
[171] McGregor, 2.

Mocenigo mustered together the finest craftsmen of the arsenal and instructed them to build a galley in "record-breaking time." Adhering to his word, a galley was indeed completed before the king could even set his fork down at breakfast the next morning.

Nonetheless, by 1510, *La Serenissima* had ceased expanding its territory and influence. Given the benefit of hindsight, it's clear this era marked the beginning of the end for the Venetian Republic, though it would hang on for two more centuries. Moreover, given its importance to the Renaissance, Venice still made unparalleled contributions to world culture, and it continued to function as a beacon to travelers who began to pour into its watery streets in order to experience a city that was still powerful, despite the fact that it was showing signs of coming apart.

Throughout the 16th century, Venice was still a large urban center, a port, a mercantile power, and an economic powerhouse, which ensured it was still quite rich.[172] As a premier tourist destination for a growing number of outsiders, Venice was full of artistic and musical festivals, and boasted an incredible archeological heritage.[173] Stores carried all sorts of jewels and spices, and unheard of fruits. Even the sophistication of their plumbing at the time earned Venice high words of praise from its early visitors.[174] Perhaps unsurprisingly given its long streak of independence, it had maintained its distance from the intellectual trends of other European nations, while still remaining an important cultural center.

In a sense, the city's prosperity allowed it to absorb major blows. Venice suffered a terrible naval defeat at Prevesa in 1538, which cost it the island of Cyprus, and it endured the plague in 1576-1577. Another crucial loss at Valeggio came in 1630, followed by the plague in 1630-1631. That said, while the city's influence was in decline, contemporary inhabitants and visitors would likely not have noticed it in real time.

Professor Jakub Grygiel of Johns Hopkins University credits the great tumble of Venice to 2 major factors – one caused by external forces, and the other, prompted by their own hand. For starters, the discovery of a fresh and much more user-friendly trade route to the Americas and the East were the granules of sand trapped in the engine of the Arsenale, triggering a stall in progress. The new trade route was preferred by many merchants, for it cut through the Atlantic and circled around Africa, circumventing the Mediterranean routes controlled by Venice and lusted after by the formidable force of the Ottoman Empire. Merchants traveling on the new route dangled slashed prices over their potential clients to bait them into shrugging off their old business flames. While a few remained loyal to their Venetian connections, many began to drop the hot potatoes that they were. It would not be long before merchants from France, Britain, Spain, Portugal, and the Netherlands closed in on them. Their competitors would soon overtake them, leaving the Venetians to inhale and navigate their way through the clouds of dust as they

---

[172] Crouzet-Pavan, "Il Rinascimento."
[173] McGregor, 3.
[174] Crouzet-Pavan, "Il Rinascimento."

struggled to keep up the pace.

The city made a clumsy attempt to pick up the pieces by hastening the assemblage of a team to build the Suez Canal towards the end of the 1500s, but the project quickly crumbled. Standing in the cold shadows of the billowing waves towering over them, it seemed as if hope was nowhere to be found. By the mid-17th century, more merchants opted for oceanic trade routes, and it became clear that the Mediterranean had lost its status as the world's leading maritime trading channel.

The other factor suggests that Venice had been instrumental in causing its own demise. Starting in the 1400s, the city shifted its neutral footing and began to flirt with Italian politics. Soon after, they embarked on a hunt for nearby territories to call their own, but it became evident that their fiery eyes far exceeded the size of their stomach. To make matters worse, the Viscontis of Milan was simultaneously flourishing, and the Milanese dream of unifying all northern Italian states was inching a step closer to reality by the day.

All the same, the city that had built itself from nothing, then proceeded to literally lift itself off the ground, was not giving up without a fight. In the early 18th century, the doors to a brand-new arsenal were opened in the Greek Island of Corfu, adding to the Venetian naval bases that already existed in Koroni, Chalkis, Chania, Heraklion, Preveza, and Methoni. The arsenal had been built as an added security measure and to boost their defense system in response to the sudden ambush of Turkish forces that infiltrated the island in 1716. The shipyard was set up to the west of the Govina Bay (the Gouvia Village today). The Govina was used as a harbor, and the arsenal constructed just by the coast of the bay. It was also conveniently situated near a dense thicket, making it easy for workers to duck into the forest to replenish their wood supplies. Behind the walls of the shipyard was a threesome of "arched docks" that catered to the 2 Venetian fleets sent over to the island shortly after the siege – one comprising a dozen "heavy sailing ships," and the other, 25 galleys, both sets fully armed.

Marc Ryckaert's picture of the ruins of the arsenal at Gouvia

However, things took a decisive turn in the mid-17th century when, against the better judgement of some, Venice went to war against the Ottoman Empire again from 1645-1669. This long war deprived Venice of Crete, the last remaining outpost in the Aegean Sea. All the Venetians had left was Dalmatia and a few Greek territories, and thanks to an alliance with the Austrians, they were able to regain some territory in the Peloponnesian islands in 1699 once the Ottomans were expelled.[175]

By the turn of the 18th century, the Venetians were back on the defensive again, as the Ottomans attacked them in Greece, winning numerous battles from 1714-1718. This conflict, which concluded with the Passarowitz Treaty, marked the end of Venetian maritime commerce in the Mediterranean, and while it ended the centuries of conflict between the Ottomans and the Venetians, it also cemented Turkish dominion over Greece. The true winner of the treaty was Austria, which was able to expand through the Balkan peninsula, a move that solidified its empire. Rather than try to regain what they had lost, Venetian politicians, following these devastating defeats, leaned heavily towards a stance of neutrality.[176]

As Venice lost its imperial influence, the cultural output remained steady. Goldoni staged his plays, and Tiepolo and Canaletto painted their masterpieces.[177] The world's most famous womanizer, Giacomo Casanova, also lived, loved, and wrote in Venice during this time, celebrating his own personal Carnevale year round.[178] The mid-18th century also marked the height of the Grand Tour, and those visitors would have found a city of music, with stripe-shirted gondoliers spontaneously bursting into song, music flowing out from open windows, groups of musicians performing for money on the streets, and bustling opera houses.[179]

Alas, the worst was yet to come. In 1797, notorious French general Napoleon Bonaparte was firmly clutching onto the crisscrossing reins in his grasp, which extended all across northern Italy, barring Venice. In the hopes of recruiting the Venetians for their help in driving the Austrians out of Italy, Napoleon addressed the city government with a passionately worded proposition: "Your whole territory is imbued with revolutionary principles. One single word from me will excite a blaze of insurrection through all your provinces. Ally yourself with France, make a few modifications in your government...and we will pacify public opinion and will sustain your authority."

At this juncture, Venice could no longer sufficiently defend itself, as its once tremendous fleet had been diminished to a pitiful fleet of 4 galleys, 7 galliots, and a smattering of scarcely sea-worthy vessels. Nonetheless, the Venetian government had rebuked Napoleon's offer and insisted

---

[175] Angione.
[176] Angione.
[177] For a recent biography of Casanova, see Laurence Bergreen, *Casanova: The World of a Seductive Genius.* (New York: Simon and Schuster, 2018).
[178] James H., Johnson. *Venice Incognito: Masks in the Serene Republic.* (Berkeley, CA: University of California Press, 2011), 3.
[179] Strathern 260, 277-8.

upon returning to the comfort of gray middle ground. Unfortunately, the feared French conqueror was not one who took kindly to rejection. What ensued explained precisely the reason 1797 has since been named the city's "annus horribilis," the Latin phrase for "horrible year."

Napoleon

Not everyone had agreed with the city's neutral stance on the French-Austria conundrum. For one, Venetian ambassador, Francesco Pesaro, had had enough. He had previously been appointed to resolve matters with Napoleon himself, but when the French general produced a manifesto with conditions that threatened Venetian independence, Pesaro vehemently and repeatedly suggested the use of force, or at the very least, to consolidate their defenses against the French.

While Pesaro gained much support from many of his peers, there were those that directed their attention to the unappealing outcomes of such a decision. Combating the crushing decline of Venice's trading industry had exhausted the city's funds. Renewing the naval fleet and other military defenses meant jacking up the taxes of the Venetian wealthy, which would only incur more unneeded fury. Beyond that, marshaling troops of their own could possibly alarm the French or Austrian leaders, or even more distressing – provoke them.

It was only in late 1796 that Pesaro's warnings were heeded and what was left of the fleet pulled back from Corfu, but their delay in action would cost them. To their dismay, all they managed to retrieve were 11 tiny and heavily outdated warships that still had some kick to them, but just barely. There was no time to build new ships, especially in an environment so steadily falling apart. Just a few weeks after the rejection of Napoleon's offer, French troops stormed into the city and headed straight for the Arsenale, pillaging the structures within the premises and slaughtering Italians along the way.

Still, a faint ray of hope pierced through the midst of the battle smoke. On October 17, 1797, after 5 years of bashing foreheads with one another, representatives from France and Austria convened to draw up an agreement of peace known as the "Treaty of Campo Fiormo." The terms of this agreement, which ended the chapter of the Italian conquest, stated that the Austrian Netherlands (now Belgium) was to be handed over to France. To even the score, France now had control over Corfu, as well as all the Italian territories on the eastern end of the Adige River, which included Istria, Friuli, Dalmatia, and last, but not least – Venice. The Republics of Liguria (better known by its previous moniker – the Republic of Genoa) and Cisalpine (territories belonging to the southern side of the Alps) were also declared independent states. It was this very treaty that sealed the city's fate, toppling an empire that lasted over 4 centuries for good.

This rocky period of instability and distorted identity would carry on well into the next century. In 1803, Napoleon proclaimed himself the King of Italy and anxiously traveled to Venice, where he published a series of reforms to reorganize the city structure and restore the glory of the Arsenale. Venice was reclassified as a "free port," meaning all imported goods to cross through the city would be exempt from taxes and duties. This helped in recreating a part of the jobs lost during the arsenal's dark ages, and resurrected business and activity within the shipyard and the Chamber of Commerce.

The city itself was given a makeover. Old buildings were scrapped and plots of land cleared out to make room for nature – namely, lush gardens, parks, a central cemetery, and other cosmetic upgrades. Welfare and corporate organizations were shut down. Compulsory conscription, or mandatory term services for young men in the military, was instituted. Certain religions were singled out and rendered illegal.

11 years later, Napoleon's Italian kingdom would be taken away from him by the Congress of Vienna. Once more, Venice was reinstated as Austrian territory under a new name – the Kingdom of Lombardy-Venetia. The new governor, Peter Goëss, picked up from where

Napoleon had left off. Apart from decreeing policies that bettered the education in Venetian primary schools, Goëss organized the construction of a railway bridge that extended across the lagoon in 1846, spiking up tourism rates and state profits accordingly.

Goëss

Visitors from near and faraway lands boarded the train for a tour of the highly-acclaimed Museo Storico Navale, or the "Naval History Museum," which had been commissioned by Goëss in 1815. On top of the Arsenale's obvious historical significance to the city, he knew that the preservation and archiving of the shipyard's legendary vessels made it a potential cash cow, one that he fully intended to milk dry. Among the most cherished artifacts that still remains in the collection today are a series of maps, delightfully yellowed with age, either illustrated or ordered by Abbot Gian Maria Maffioletti. These full-color, meticulously labeled maps are said to be the only existing diagrams depicting the Arsenale before its fall, and is particularly prized for its exquisite level of detail.

Although the Austrian reign had contributed to the gradual restoration of the city's wealth, the Venetians never took to the foreigner on the throne. In 1848, Venetians became the first to take a stab at the fight for Italian independence. A violent mob, recruited by a group of local scholars and patriots, barged into the state prison, disarmed the guards, and snuck out the captive, Daniele Manin, in the thick of the chaos. Manin, one of the key figures of the Risorgimento, the name given to the movement behind the liberation and unification of Italy, introduced his own brand of government 5 days later.

Manin

Though Manin's overambitious endeavors fizzled out about a year later, their victories, however small, had instilled in the nation an invigorated will to resist. On March 23, 1848, the King of Sardinia, Carlo Alberto of Savoy, declared war against Austria, kicking off the first of the Italian Wars of Independence. At long last, on October 21, 1866, Venice was annexed to the Kingdom of Italy, headed by the Savoy Monarchy.

Venetian history is as unwieldy and hard to define as the mysterious city itself. From its humble origins as a place of asylum for fleeing refugees to its glory days as a rival to the world's greatest empires, Venice's past does not consist of one story so much as it does many competing, knotty narratives that confound historians to this day. For all the complicated twists and turns, it seems fair to conclude that the far-reaching influence held by Venice was due to its unparalleled entrepreneurial drive and its extraordinary ability to organize. That same boundless energy produced spectacular buildings and unique art, music, and theater.[180] Over time, Venice produced its own rich literary and artistic production, boasting writers such as Matteo Bandello and Carlo Goldoni, as well as painters such as Tintoretto and Titian. As much as it engaged with the Italian city states to the south, it also had a dynamic relationship with Germany and Austria to the north. One of the largest cities in Europe, it nonetheless was always in conversation with the East, giving it a distinctly cosmopolitan sensibility.

As the centuries of the Republic of Venice become ever more distant, its legacy appears no less shiny than it was during its glory years, and due to its importance, Venice is also experiencing a substantial scholarly Renaissance, with new and exciting research currently being done on a regular basis thanks to the empire's scholarly archives - hastily packed away after the French conquest in 1797 - being available once again for scholars. Today, historical research tends to look at the city's long-term civic success, its vastly lucrative commercial empire, and its unparalleled dominance in the Mediterranean.[181]

The Decline of Genoa's Republic

Shortly after the death of Andrea Doria, Liguria was hit by a series of hardships, most problematically a number of bad harvests between 1586 and 1590. This was particularly onerous for Liguria, which already had difficulty with food supplies because of its barren landscape. Since their loss of most of their eastern Mediterranean colonies during the previous century, the Genoese depended on the Spanish to guarantee their food supply in exchange for services provided by their fleets and their banks.[182] These crop failures sent Genoa into a state of confusion as they tried a number of solutions, including efforts to stimulate their grain production, efforts to reassert their maritime dominance (in the hopes of either intercepting or escorting grain shipments), and efforts to attract foreign grain merchants to the city. They even attempted to stimulate cereal production in their Corsican territory by giving Genoese citizens fiefs to cultivate, but this initiative does not seem to have yielded the desired increase.[183] As a result, this disparate strategy of military and commercial elements brought about a major financial strain on the city, precipitating a full-blown crisis.[184]

After the end of the Genoa's golden age, the 17th century was a transitional time for the Republic that ultimately brought a period of progressive decline. In response to Spanish insolvency, Genoa attempted to regroup and find alternatives to its relationship with Spain. In the first 30 years of the century, they slowly withdrew themselves from the Spanish court and exhibited a desire to maintain neutrality by keeping a political and diplomatic distance from their former ally.[185] However, despite this desire to maintain neutrality, Genoa faced aggressions on

---

[180] McGregor, 5.
[181] Crouzet-Pavan, *Venice Triumphant*, ix.
[182] Kirk, 152-153. See also Grendi, *La Repubblica Aristocratica Dei Genovesi*, 172-223.
[183] Kirk, 156.
[184] Kirk, 153-4.
[185] Kirk, 84-5.

the part of France that continued to increase in intensity over the years. In 1639, the French gained control of a Genoese ship in nearby San Remo, and the next year they captured eight merchant ships in transit in the sea of Liguria. During this time, Genoa continued to demonstrate its allegiance to the Spanish, allowing their ships to take refuge in their port when they were being pursued by a fleet of French ships, but it had become clear that the Genoese could not rely on the Spanish for protection, so they attempted to create a new armament, manned by free, paid oarsman (as opposed to slaves). This armament would be like an emergency defense system comprised of 12 ships, doubling their previous defenses, but the production only sustained itself for about six months. By July 1641, funds for the project had been exhausted, requiring the levying of taxes on citizens to try to make up the difference.

While there was increasing international competition with the other naval powers of Europe, the Republic's commercial activities progressed.[186] Luckily, efforts to build commercial ships were more successful, even as the Genoese faced the constant threat of Barbary pirates in the waters nearby Corsica and Sardinia.[187] Most remarkably, as the state was about to fall to pieces, some elite Genoese looking for even bolder new opportunities formed the Compagnia Genovese Delle Indie Orientali. This company sought to imitate the Dutch and establish trade in the East, specifically in Japan (although this extravagant promise might simply have been a marketing ploy). The timing of such a venture seemed right, as their competitors were all tied up in other conflicts. France, Spain, and the United Provinces were entrenched in the Thirty Years' War, Portugal was just barely shaking off the Spanish, and England was roiled by civil war.

There was even an expectation of Dutch acceptance of the venture, but this proved to be misguided. The company's ships set sail in March, 1648, but 11 months later they were captured by the Dutch, who confiscated them, their merchandise, and all their money, bringing to an end the short audacious venture.[188] The fact that the Dutch enjoyed such a strong reputation at this time meant that there was little that Genoa could do by way of retaliation. After attempting to recoup losses diplomatically, the Genoese came up short and simply accepted the losses.[189]

It was against this backdrop that another blow hit the Republic in 1652, when Genoa was hit by another serious outbreak of the plague. Whereas details about the Black Death of 1348 remain sketchy so far as Genoa is concerned, historians are fairly confident in estimating that this plague was responsible for the deaths of approximately 700 people per day.[190] As a result of this plague, the economic life of the city was disrupted, and even the charitable institutions were closed down when most would have been needed.[191] As a response to this disaster, one wealthy, virtuous

---

[186] Brilli, 1.
[187] Kirk, 118.
[188] Kirk, 129-130.
[189] Kirk, 130. Impressively enough, however, further ventures were planned in the wake of this failure, including a plan to send ships to Brazil in 1659, thanks to funding from the Casa di San Giorgio. This venture also failed, and foreshadowed the fact that the sun had set on the Genoese empire. Kirk, 131-2.
[190] Walton, 24. Approximately 10,000 victims were found in a mass grave just outside the city walls.
[191] Walton, 24.

Genoese man, Emanuele Brignole, founded the Albergo dei Poveri in 1658 (literally the hotel of the poor). The construction of the building aimed to offer employment to the poor in exchange for food and shelter.[192]

Brignole

As good as Brignole's intentions were, they were ultimately perverted in their execution. In fact, rather than being a charitable venture, the creation of the Albergo dei Poveri instead marked the birth of a prototypical workhouse. More or less, it served as a prison complex that housed those infected with syphilis, those deemed insane, and beggars, orphans, criminals and vagabonds who refused to work. In essence, it was home to those that society had chosen to reject, and in the Albergo dei Poveri, these social outcasts were put to work making cheap cloth and clothing. In 1664, there were over 1,000 inmates and incarcerated slaves, while other slaves were entrusted with supervising the inmates. Even more unfortunately, this misery was not confined to the city of Genoa, as Emanuele Brignole's workhouse ended up influencing

---

[192] Walton, 24. Remarkably, the Albergo survived until 2012 when the last eighty residents moved into other hospitals. Today, the university is tasked with taking charge of the Albergo and restoring it to its former (intended) charitable use. Walton, 28.

workhouses throughout Europe.[193]

The Ospedale L'Albergo Reale dei Poveri in Naples

Genoa was not able to restore itself this time, and in 1684, King Louis XIV of France set his sights on the city.[194] On May 17, 1684, the French fleet entered the harbor and gave the Genoese Senate five hours to decide whether to surrender. When the Genoese responded with cannon fire, the French replied with a devastating barrage of firepower, and the Genoese soon realized they were outmatched. In four days, the French fired 6,000 shots at the city, and they promised to fire 10,000 more if the Genoese did not surrender. Over the course of the next week, the French proceeded to empty its arsenal on Genoa, hitting about a third of the city's houses and completely destroying half of those. The city looked like it had been struck by an earthquake, with smoking cinders and mangled bodies everywhere. Observers reported a stench in the air as the water pipes and sewage drains were struck, allowing foul liquids to seep forth.[195]

---

[193] Epstein, 320-1.
[194] Anonymous, *Genoa*, 42.
[195] Carden, 142-143.

A depiction of the bombardment of Genoa in 1684

The French left, but the Genoese found themselves diplomatically isolated. Within a year, they were forced to send an envoy to Versailles to humiliate themselves before the French court. From this point on, the Republic of Genoa would find itself ever more beholden to France.[196] The French bombardment also had a physical impact on the space of the city along with the Republic's diplomatic agenda - a traveler to Genoa in the early 1700s remarked with horror at the squalid conditions of the city and its decimated naval capacity.[197]

---

[196] "Genova," *Enciclopedia Treccani.* Treccani.it, Accessed April 17, 2019.
[197] Anonymous, *Genoa,* 42-43.

The Doge of Genoa at Versailles on 15 May 1685, **by Claude Guy Halle**

Despite the negative impression of these early travelers to Genoa, the city was about to become an obligatory stop on the Grand Tour thanks to the completion of the Strada Nuova ("New Street") in 1716.[198] Indeed, despite being somewhat off the beaten track, Genoa found words of affection from its visitors (even if these are not the same jaw-dropping odes elicited by the rival city of Venice). Tourists' first impressions were often negative as they were confronted by the swarming urban chaos, but people came to appreciate the beautiful architecture found all around them.[199] The 18th century Jesuit Italian poet Saverio Bettinelli had these verses to dedicate to Genoa: "Behold the city majestic and vast, / Sea at her feet, and mountain at her back, / Filling all space between the shore and height, / And filling it all with beauty."[200] In his travelogue *Italy Revisited,* the great American novelist Henry James described it with intense, though somewhat critical words, writing, "Genoa, as I have hinted, is the crookedest and most incoherent of cities; tossed about on the sides and crests of a dozen hills, it is seamed with gullies and ravines that bristle with those innumerable palaces for which we have heard from our earliest years that the place is celebrated."[201] In *Pictures from Italy,* the great British novelist Charles Dickens wrote, "It is a place that 'grows upon you' every day. There seems to find out in it."[202]

---

[198] Walton, xiv.
[199] Walton, 112, 114.
[200] Anonymous, *Genoa*, 1.
[201] Henry James, *Italian Hours* (Boston and New York: Houghton Mifflin, 1909). For a contemporary Dutch novel set in the present-day city of Genoa, that gives an authentic feel of the city's vibe, see Ilja Pfeijffer, *La Superba* (Dallas, TX: Deep Vellum Publishing, 2016).
[202] Charles Dickens, *Christmas Stories and Pictures from Italy* (London: Getz, Buck & Company, 1852). Somewhat less complimentary, he also referred to it as "a bewildering phantasmagoria." See Walton, 1. Beyond the poetry it inspired by foreigners, Genoa was also known as a destination for sexual tourism, for those seeking both female and

In the 18th century, Genoa attempted a policy of cautious neutrality toward its strongest neighbors, which included Spain, France, Austria, and Sardinia. This was all but necessary since those powers were all showing signs of expansion, but in 1746, Genoa was sacked by the Austrians. Genoa faced foreign rule for a brief time before a popular revolt overthrew the Austrian overlords.[203]

In 1768, Genoa finally ceded control of their valuable territory of Corsica, where they had been facing constant uprisings. This was a necessary decision that seemed to be in the best interest of Genoa, which was no longer able to keep together a fraying empire. In turn, Corsica because it was freed of the harsh Genoese rule.[204]

As fate would have it, Genoa sold Corsica to the French just months before a young boy named Napoleon was born on the island. Less than 30 years later, Napoleon headed to Italy in command of the Army of Italy and launched an all-out invasion across the Alps in 1796. Austria's capitulation to Napoleon signaled the end of the Italian cities' independence. In 1797, the Republic of Genoa ceased to exist, extinguished the very same year the Republic of Venice was destroyed. The ancient aristocratic republics were transformed into democratic republics under the heavy thumb of the French.

Despite the loss of autonomy, Genoese commercial activities still were able to continue, even after the invasion of Napoleon closed the Casa di San Giorgio.[205] This persistence serves as a testament to just how ingrained commerce was for Genoese society, and how organized their mercantile and maritime endeavors had been.[206]

Unfortunately, the people's resilience didn't matter much, because Genoa's status in the French Empire ensured that Liguria became a target of Napoleon's enemies. The region faced maritime and land attacks by the British, and after Napoleon was decisively defeated at Waterloo in 1815, Genoa was annexed by the Sardinian kingdom, ruled by the Piedmontese.[207]

Genoa would take on an entirely new role in the early 19th century, but it still found itself at the forefront of global events. A major expedition in the war for Italian Unification set sail from Genoa in 1860, and after Italy was unified, Genoa became one of the main ports through which Italians journeyed on their way to becoming immigrants in the Americas.[208] Describing the city in the early 19th century, writers still felt a certain intimidation when approaching the rocky territory, its illustrious history, and its famously closed people. It was clear the pride of Genoa

---

male companionship—although Dickens had rather harsh words for the women of Genoa whom he said reminded him of witches, Walton 114-5.
[203] Epstein, 321.
[204] Walton, 124.
[205] Walton, xiv.
[206] Brilli, 1.
[207] Brilli, 137.
[208] Walton, xv.

had not been sapped away by the French, even if the city now contained large areas with impoverished people and squalid living conditions.

Indeed, Genoa still has a reputation for being one of the least understood cities in Italy.[209] As one writer noted, in order to understand Genoa, it is not enough to arrive there with a guidebook in hand. Perhaps such preparation is sufficient in learning about the artistic treasures of the city, but to understand the people and their character, visitors must spend months or even years immersing themselves in the culture. This is particularly true in the English-speaking world, even as Westerners continue to show avid interest in everything about Italy.

Indeed, the city continues to prominently affect the world even as few people know of its major contributions to culture. Blue jeans came from Genoa (the French pronounced the city's name as *Genes*, and Genoa is where the cloth originated), and Genoa gives its name to a special kind of salami. Christopher Columbus hailed from Genoa, as did one of the world's greatest violinists, Niccolo Paganini, and one of the heroes of Italian Unification, Giuseppe Mazzini.[210] Genoa today boasts a population of just over 580,000 people,[211] people who have collectively earned a reputation as proud and independent people.

The history of Genoa is not about single individuals, nor can it be told in isolation. Instead, it illuminates a major piece of history over the last millennium. Hemmed in by natural features on all sides, this powerful naval and commercial commonwealth was only ever able to occupy a miniscule speck of Europe, but nonetheless, thanks to its colonies and its powerful system of banking, Genoa spread its influence over the entire West.[212]

At the same time, while celebrating its status as a major port city, its other historical and cultural contributions should not be overlooked.[213] Its museums are worthy of a tourist's interest, and its historic center boasts a maze of alleys with dizzying staircases and streets so narrow that a person can touch both sides at once.[214] Nor is Genoa simply resting on the laurels of its past glory, as modern updates by prestigious Italian architects such as Renzo Piano have restored parts of the city's past by integrating them with modern updates.[215]

Genoa has long been at the forefront of major forces that shaped events across continents, for better or worse. In the Middle Ages, it was Genoa that helped shepherd in the age of capitalism, which prominently featured slavery and colonization. In the 16th century, Genoa led the rise in international public finance, and in the 17th century it led the way in finding new ways to provide relief to the impoverished. In the 19th century, republicanism found a firm foothold in Genoa, but

---

[209] Carlo Bitossi, *Repubblica Di Genova* (Corsica, France: F.M. Ricci, 1996), 11.
[210] Epstein, *Genoa and the Genoese, 958-1528*, xiii.
[211] "Genova," Enciclopedia Treccani. Treccani.it, Accessed April 17, 2019.
[212] Bent, v.
[213] Benes, "Introduction," 1.
[214] Robert Walter Carden, *The City of Genoa* (Genoa: Methuen, 1908), v.
[215] Benes, "Introduction," 1.

the city was also one of the early strongholds of fascism in the 20th century.[216]

What the future holds for Italy is hard to say, but perhaps the place to look for answers is its proudest city.

Online Resources

Other medieval history titles by Charles River Editors & Sean McLachlan

Other titles about Venice on Amazon

Bibliography

Ambrosini, Federica. "Toward a Social History of Women in Venice. From the Renaissance to the Enlightenment." In *Venice Reconsidered. The History and Civilization of an Italian City-State, 1297-1797,* edited by John Martin and Dennis Romano. Baltimore, MD and London: The Johns Hopkins University Press, 2000, 420-453.

Bosworth, Richard J.B., *Italian Venice: A History.* New Haven, CT: Yale University Press, 2014.

Chambers, D.S. *The Imperial Age of Venice* (1380-1580). London: Harcourt Brace Jovanovich, inc., 1970.

Crouzet-Pavan, Elisabeth. *Venice Triumphant: The Horizons of a Myth*. Translated by Lydia G. Cochrane. (Baltimore, MD: The Johns Hopkins University Press, 2005).

---. "Il Rinascimento. Politica e cultura. La cultura: Immagini di un mito." Translated by Matteo Sanfilippo. In *Enciclopedia Treccani,* treccani.it. Accessed April 6, 2019.

---. "Toward and Ecological Understanding of the Myth of Venice." In *Venice Reconsidered. The History and Civilization of an Italian City-State, 1297-1797,* edited by John Martin and Dennis Romano. Baltimore, MD and London: The Johns Hopkins University Press, 2000, 39-66.

Crowley, Roger. *City of Fortune: How Venice Ruled the Seas.* New York: Random House, 2012.

Dursteler, Eric R., *A Companion to Venetian History,* 1400-1797. Boston, MA: Leiden, 2013.

Ferraro, Joanne M. *Venice: history of the Floating City.* New York: Cambridge University Press, 2012.

---

[216] Epstein, *Genoa and the Genoese, 958-1528*, xiv.

Fusaro, Maria. *A Short History of Venice and the Venetian Empire,* London: I.B. Tauris, Limited, 2007.

Hill, Reginald. *Another Death in Venice.* London: The Crime Club, 1976.

Horodowich, Elizabeth. *A Brief History of Venice: A New History of the City and Its People.* New York: Little Brown Book Group, 2013.

Johnson, James H., *Venice Incognito: Masks in the Serene Republic.* Berkeley, CA: University of California Press, 2011.

Lane, Frederic C. *Venice: A Maritime Republic.* Baltimore and London: The Johns Hopkins University Press, 1973.

Longworth, Philip. *The Rise and Fall of Venice.* London: Constable, 1974.

Madden, Thomas F., *Venice: A New History.* New York: Penguin Books, 2012.

-- "Venice's Hostage Crisis: Diplomatic Efforts to Secure Peace with Byzantium between 1171 and 1184." In *Medieval and Renaissance Venice,* edited by Ellen E. Kittell and Thomas F. Madden. Urbana, IL: University of Illinois Press, 1999: 97-108.

Martin, John and Romano, Dennis. "Preface." In *Venice Reconsidered. The History and Civilization of an Italian City-State, 1297-1797,* edited by John Martin and Dennis Romano. Baltimore, MD and London: The Johns Hopkins University Press, 2000, ix-xiii.

---."Reconsidering Venice, " In *Venice Reconsidered. The History and Civilization of an Italian City-State, 1297-1797,* edited by John Martin and Dennis Romano. Baltimore, MD and London: The Johns Hopkins University Press, 2000, 1-38.

McNeill, William H. *Venice: The Hinge of Europe,* 1081-1797. Chicago, IL: University of Chicago Press, 2009.

Morris, Jan. *The Venetian Empire: A Sea Voyage.* London: Penguin, 1990.

Muir, Edward, "Was There Republicanism in The Renaissance Republics? Venice after Agnadello," In *Venice Reconsidered. The History and Civilization of an Italian City-State, 1297-1797,* edited by John Martin and Dennis Romano. Baltimore, MD and London: The Johns Hopkins University Press, 2000, 137-167.

Nicol, Donald M. *Byzantium and Venice: A Study in Diplomatic and Cultural Relations.* Cambridge, MA: Cambridge University Press, 1992.

Norwich, John Julius. *Venice: The Rise to Empire.* London: Allen Lane, 1977.

O'Connell, Monique. *Men of Empire: Power and Negotiation in Venice's Maritime State.* Baltimore, MD: Johns Hopkins University Press, 2009.

Preto, Paolo. "Dal Rinascimento al Barocco – La Societa`: Le 'paure' della società Veneziana: Le calamità, le sconfitte, i nemici esterni," Encyclopedia Treccani, Treccani.it. Accessed April 6, 2019.

Rothman, E. Natalie. *Brokering Empire: Trans-Imperial Subjects between Venice and Istanbul.* Ithaca, NY: Cornell University Press, 2012.

Scarpa, Tiziano. *Venezia è un pesce. Una guida.* Milan: Giangiacomo Feltrinelli Editore, 2000.

Strathern, Paul. *The Spirit of Venice. From Marco Polo to Casanova.* London: Jonathan Cape, 2012.

"Venezia," Treccani, it. Accessed April 6, 2019

Wills, Garry. *Venice: Lion City: The Religion of Empire.* New York: Simon and Schuster, 2013.

Free Books by Charles River Editors

We have brand new titles available for free most days of the week. To see which of our titles are currently free, click on this link.

Discounted Books by Charles River Editors

We have titles at a discount price of just 99 cents everyday. To see which of our titles are currently 99 cents, click on this link.

Made in the USA
Middletown, DE
14 June 2019